Advanced Praise for *A Whole New Life*

"Wow! This is the most insightful and profound book on life and change in many many years. Clear observations, wise insights and un-judging tone, sprinkled with amazing quotes and relatable anecdotes. Very powerful. Highly recommended."

—Derek Sivers, sivers.org

"I have known Lucia for quite some years now, and have always been shocked at her ability of putting complex situations in a very simple frame. Her multidisciplinary knowledge and training always push you to view from different perspectives through an extremely balanced approach, thus realizing where you are and the blocks that pull you back. Her wisdom in making things easy allow you to see change as a mere exercise, no more an insurmountable task. Her friendship and support have been extremely important in evaluating complicated situations."

—Alessandro Giuliani, Managing Director, MISB Bocconi, India

"*A Whole New Life*—is a powerful journey that takes us from awareness to action. In our experience, the true key to change, is to be able to have access to different tools, that one can reach out to, whenever life comes calling. This book provides exactly that! A guide to help us year after year, to create our life of our dreams!

"Lucia has offered several courses in India, and *A Whole New Life* is an instant hit. It helps participants go deeper in their understanding of themselves, dissolving barriers and blocks and creating a powerful vision. Months after the seminar, participants have written to us, sharing how her techniques are helping them. It is overwhelming.

"Lucia's insights and intuitive ability to understand people, creates an instant connection with her readers. Her genius lies in making complex things, simple. Her passion for creating change and her understanding of psychology comes through in every touch point. This book is truly a pathway to creating a whole new life!"

—Sneha Shah & Shashank Gupta, Directors, ISRA

A WHOLE NEW LIFE

DISCOVER THE POWER OF
POSITIVE TRANSFORMATION

Lucia Giovannini

A POST HILL PRESS BOOK

ISBN: 978-1-64293-043-6
ISBN (eBook): 978-1-64293-044-3

A Whole New Life:
Discover the Power of Positive Transformation
© 2019 by Lucia Giovannini
All Rights Reserved

Cover design by Cody Corcoran

Post Hill Press, LLC
New York • Nashville
posthillpress.com

Published in the United States of America

Rosanna and Renato,
if you don't already know it (because maybe
I've never expressed it clearly enough), you have
been two wonderful parents. Thank you for having accompanied me on this journey on Earth and
for never having stopped believing in me.

Nicola,
thank you for your love and for your presence in
my life. Your support is precious and the simple fact
that you are by my side makes me feel at home.

CONTENTS

AUTHOR'S NOTE

To better illustrate the proposed concepts, I have chosen to share many personal anecdotes and actual cases involving people who have participated in our corporate meetings or public courses during the last ten years. In order to protect their privacy, names and significant details have been changed. The episodes related to my own life, however, are true to life because my intent is to share my personal journey toward change and its relative lessons in their entirety.

FOREWORD

Within every human heart there is a yearning to find meaning and purpose in life, to somehow make a difference on the earth. That desire within you is why you were drawn to this book. Sometimes, the search begins with feelings of unhappiness or a vague sense that there is a depth of life you haven't yet touched. Other times it's a sudden, unexpected challenge like losing a job, relationship, finances, or health that is the beginning of an inner examination of oneself and life.

Be comforted. *A Whole New Life* is the guide you have been looking for. The author provides a roadmap to changes on every level of life: physical, mental, emotional, and spiritual. It inspires you to say *yes* to your life and your dreams, the passions and the possibilities. Are you willing to take the journey? A roadmap doesn't do any good unless you are willing to embark on the road. All it takes is your willingness to get started, and a commitment to each step of the process.

We humans often say we want to change our lives. Why don't we? Perhaps we lack the skills needed to embrace change, or the ego brings up the fear of the unknown, a new path where the end is not in sight. What will it take to go on this path? As a therapist, I have worked with people who were dissatisfied with a job or relationship, and despite the change work we did, they stayed stuck in the situation. Until...one day they were fired, or their partner decided to leave. When we don't follow the whispers of our heart, they get louder. If we still don't make the change, spirit has a way of creating what we say we want in a way we never expected.

Our life stories begin forming at a very young age. The unconscious mind absorbs all our experiences, the words we hear from others and the emotions we feel in response. It tucks them all away and installs beliefs about future experiences. We begin to create stories in our heads about our worthiness to receive love, our potential success in life (or lack of it), whether change is safe or scary, what money we can earn, and so many more! Then our unconscious mind does its best to recreate these stories in our adult life. During training workshops, I teach in Louise Hay's philosophy, I use a pair of oversized sunglasses to demonstrate how we all have filters (oh, so many of them!) in the unconscious mind that block us from achieving our potential and living an empowered life in all areas. Especially in the area of relationships, the participants can easily understand (and sometimes even laugh about) how many of the differences with their partners occur because of these filters. Awareness of the filters in all areas of our lives is the key to positive change.

Imagine for a moment, the many sunglasses you walk around with every day. Each one is filtering your experience, taking in what you already believe about yourself, keeping out what you don't. Your daily thought patterns are creating emotions that enact the childhood beliefs. For the next few days, act as an observer of your own mind. Pay close attention to your thoughts—are these thoughts empowering you or not? *A Whole New Life* shows you step by step how to take off the sunglasses and achieve your dreams.

Yes, stepping out into new territory can be scary. It takes courage and trust. I am reminded of a riveting scene in the movie, *Indiana Jones and the Last Crusade*. Indiana is on a quest for the Holy Grail (the chalice Jesus drank from at the Last Supper). The quest becomes truly urgent when Indiana's father is shot, and only the water from the Grail will save him. Using a small book with ambiguous clues, Indiana passes two obstacles and arrives at the third, a huge crevice resembling the Grand Canyon. His only clue is to "leap from the lion's head." To do so appears to be falling to his death in the abyss. His inner struggle is apparent as the camera shows the close-up of his face. Does he trust the clue and leap or not? Suddenly, he leaps! Incredibly, there is a bridge he lands on that was invisible before.

Life is like this. Spirit always has a safety net waiting for us, although in the midst of a challenge, it can be difficult to trust that there is a solution. And yet, the key is focusing on what you want, not what you are experiencing. Remember that what you resist persists. Miracles happen when you are trusting there is some solution for the challenge you're facing or some new path you are choosing, despite not knowing how it will happen. Most people have an old pattern of obsessing about the problem rather than ordering the solution from what I playfully like to call the Cosmic Kitchen. What are your life's orders?

As you go through each chapter in this book you will discover powerful ideas and examples to help you develop a deeper level of trust in yourself. As you put the ideas into practice, you will understand the process of change for yourself, and what has been holding you back. You will discover what inspires you to action, and how to use tools like meditation, breathing techniques, and vision maps to transform your life.

Lucia Giovannini has masterfully brought together her unique personal experiences, examples of her clients' paths of change, scientific studies, a variety of personal growth processes, thought provoking ideas and questions, practical tools for transformation, and much more to inspire you with the possibilities for your life.

Nurture the new ideas, emotions and patterns. No one else can achieve your dreams. Those dreams are in your heart for a reason, and life is there to support you as you step out in trust and courage to fulfill them.

—Patricia J. Crane, Ph.D.
Author, Ordering from the Cosmic Kitchen: The Essential Guide to Powerful, Nourishing Affirmations and Master Trainer for the Heal Your Life Workshop Leader Training in Louise Hay's philosophy.

PREFACE

Until recently, if someone had asked me, "What is *A Whole New Life?*" I would have answered: It's a guide to change. And, in effect, it is. For years, *A Whole New Life* has helped thousands of readers create desired changes in their lives, achieve their own dreams or, at least, make great progress toward those ends. At the same time, it has supported an equal number of people to better manage undesired changes that life has sent them.

So, yes, the book in your hands is a guide to change. But, since its first printing, I have realized that it is much more! *A Whole New Life* is a way of gathering forty years of my personal experience of spiritual and psychological research along with more than twenty years of teaching. It unites my transformation story to the stories of many participants in the BlessYou seminars around the world. It gathers various techniques and current philosophies and is a bridge between East and West, between logic and intuition, between ancient wisdom, modern scientific discoveries and future possibilities.

When you begin to put it into practice, you will find that it is a lifestyle. *A Whole New Life* is first a promise, then an idea, a series of steps and, in the end, a reality.

INTRODUCTION

The difference between what we accomplish and what we are capable of accomplishing would resolve most of the problems of the world.

—Mahatma Gandhi

Often the participants at my weekend seminars ask me: "What books do you recommend that we should read?"

And then comes the big question: "Why don't you write a book that would help us to use the steps toward our personal growth in our daily lives and accelerate our change. It would be like having a personal coach by our side at all times."

For years, my answer was automatic: "There are thousands of books. Here's a list of the interesting ones." But every time someone would ask the question, something made my heart beat and my eyes twinkle. Evidently, the call was deep.

A thought, however, crept into my mind: "Who do you think you are? What's so special about you to make you think you can write a book that could actually help people?"

In July 2005, my husband Nicola and I had planned a trip to the United States to attend a series of lectures, but, at the last minute, the plan changed. All of a sudden, I had a great resource on my hands: time. And I had a lot of it. There were no more excuses. Finally, I had the time to start the book that I'd always wanted to write.

Despite this, after a couple of days, I found myself full of commitments. I had to finish decorating the house we had just moved to; I had to work in the garden; I had to update my website. Of course, my goal was still in front of me, but there was always something to stop me from taking the leap, to start writing. The space that separated me from what I wished for seemed enormous, so enormous that I seriously considered abandoning the idea. After all, it was only a dream. And besides, it was hard to even think of achieving it.

It's too complicated, I thought; I don't have enough time (or resources or money or ability), I will never be able to do it!

Does it sound familiar? How many times have you said the same thing?

I knew what I wanted, but, even so, it wasn't easy. How many of us can honestly say that we know exactly what we want? And, moreover, how can we connect what we want with our reason for living? What are the stages of change and in which order should we put them? And how can we learn to accept forced changes, the ones that life gives us? How can we transform uncertainty, pain and suffering into fuel for our personal growth?

These and many other questions have been with me for many years and have pushed me to analyze the implications of the human soul, to study the newest discoveries in cognitive psychology and neurology, and to examine ancient spiritual writings; to speak with men and women of medicine in the remotest parts of the world and to experiment—on myself—with all that I learned while I met the changes in my life and the large and small challenges that they brought.

These and others are the questions that will be discussed in the following pages, with the idea of guiding you toward change.

* * *

WHO THIS BOOK IS WRITTEN FOR, WHAT IS IT ABOUT AND RESULTS YOU CAN EXPECT

> *We don't know if changing is better, but we know that to get better, we must change.*
>
> —*Anonymous*

Basically, the problems that we face in life can be put in two categories: the ones that obligate us to change against our will and the changes that we desire but we don't get.

In the second case, the possibilities are two: we know what we want but we don't know how to get it—or we don't know what we want.

Whether you are faced with a change that you did not choose or you have a dream that you do wish for: you are about to start a new phase of life; you want it to be better, to develop your potential; you want your life to assume a deeper and more satisfying meaning. In any case, these pages intend to guide you during the transformation. *A Whole New Life* is intended to be a solid aid in helping you find the motivation, the strength and the tools to face and resolve difficult situations. The book talks about dreams and teaches you how to make them come true. It will teach you how to develop flexibility without losing direction.

It will take you through various stages of change: the conscious decision to initiate change; the acknowledgment of the mechanisms that we use to anesthetize ourselves against emotional pain and which prevent us from fully listening to the call of change. It is an invitation to take a look at the direction that our lives are taking, a push to boost our self-realization and a guide for making a "map of the vision." Once completed, we'll have a compass to better guide our emotions and moods and to give us a new direction for our actions.

This book will also teach us some techniques, easy and available to all, that can be compared to a virtual tool box. Once you have them, you will have them at your disposition for your whole life, without an expiration date! Over many years, during my seminars, I've had the honor of witnessing change in thousands of people, who, thanks to these journeys, have notably improved their quality of life, their relationships and their work.

Obviously, it is not, and does not want to be, a magic pill that will resolve all your problems. It is a book where you will find the seeds, learn how to plant them, take care of them and get the fruits that you hope for. This process requires willingness, commitment and action.

It has happened to thousands of people all over the world. It happened to me, and it is for this reason that I decided to share parts of my life with you. Why shouldn't it work for you, too?

SUGGESTIONS FOR USE

> *To feel full, you must cook and eat. If you want fruit to grow, studying agriculture is not enough. You must plant the trees and take care of them.*
>
> *—Mata Amritanandamayi (Amma)*

There are various ways to use this book. My suggestion is to first read it through right to the end and you will reap many benefits. You'll get new ideas, new knowledge and possibly deepen some concepts that you already were familiar with. Then you can reread the book and apply the key questions of each chapter to your own life and see what happens. This way you will have a true and real interior journey, a journey toward a new relationship with yourself and the world.

You will find various exercises that will guide you through the steps of transformation and then, because the quality of our life is almost completely determined by the quality of the questions that we ask ourselves, you will also find many questions. If you answer honestly, new possibilities will open; you will get to know yourself better. As we will see, a lot of what guides our thoughts and reactions happens at the unconscious level, without our even realizing it. The questions that you find in the various chapters have been created exactly to help you see this part of yourself. If you are confused by some, don't worry. It only means that the mechanisms are still in your unconscious. To become aware of them, you will use a technique that we suggest at our classes; you will ask yourself, "I know that I don't know, but, if I knew, what would my answer be?" and let yourself simply think and let ideas emerge, without trying to judge or change them.

In all my seminars, the experimental part has a very important role: only through experience can we find what is true for us and then completely and deeply absorb it. There's a big difference between intellectual knowledge and the emotional. Knowing how to relax, produces an effect completely different from having a relaxing experience. In the same way, the exercises that you find in these pages will help train your mental muscles, emotional and spiritual. And they can be done alone, with a friend or in groups.

In addition, something that can help strengthen your relationship with this book is to keep a diary. When you begin your internal journey, it is very useful to take notes about your thoughts and your moods, your reactions, your dreams and any deep intuitions that you may have. All of this will help you to put down on paper your personal story and to be more aware of what is happening to you. On my website www.luciagiovannini.com, you will find many resources, articles, photos, experiences, additional exercises and, in the blog, you can contact other readers in the world to discuss about what I love to call "the path of change."

You can, of course, do the same thing without a paper and a pen, but you would lose your train of thought. The act of writing down the ideas allows the mind to clear itself of its thousand crowded thoughts and to detach itself from emotion and worry. You can retrace your path of change and your exercises over and over. Use it as a guide whenever you want to make a change in some area of your life. For this to work, it is not necessary for you to accept it blindfolded or that you must agree with every idea that is presented. Even if, in the end, you make yours only one idea or one exercise, it will make a difference in your life.

As we grow, it does not take a lot to help us reach physical independence; a healthy diet along with exercise usually makes us reach this state . naturally. But can we say the same of psychological and emotional independence? Is that as easy to attain?

How much do we know about what happens within ourselves? Most people dedicate a lot of energy, time and money to improve their outer self, but is that enough to confront the challenges of life? How much time do we dedicate to knowing and improving ourselves? How would our lives change if we accepted the idea of trying just as hard to exercise for our mental and emotional well-being?

I think that it's time to invest in real well-being and to dedicate a little time and energy exploring our internal mechanisms and the complexity of our mind-body-emotions systems.

Are you willing to train your heart and your mind?

Do you want to enter the circuit of change?

Bon Voyage!
Lucia

CHAPTER 1

EMBRACING CHANGE

It's not the strongest or the most intelligent of the species that survive but those who adapt best to change.

—*Charles Darwin*

There are certain conditions or assumptions that are necessary to verify a positive transformation. And there are different levels on which this transformation can occur. What you are about to read is the result of experience, study, analysis and research of human behavior when confronted with change, regardless of whether the change is forced by what life deals us or improvements that we choose ourselves. Recognizing these levels of change, you will more deeply understand the process of transformation and will be able to develop the behaviors and feelings necessary to best start your journey.

In the following chapters, we will build solid foundations, create a base that will be enriched, developed, built and reinforced with examples, explanations and exercises. I will talk to you about the paradoxes of change. Meeting with the contradictions of the paradoxes can leave much unsaid. The reality is actually embracing two extreme realities in apparent contrast between them so it will increase our point of view, and we will create the space for the change to exist. I don't know if you have noticed, but life itself is full of paradoxes. An example is the ability to remain faithful to oneself, to one's values, to one's own personal ethics, and, at the same time, be able to modify one's own beliefs.

THE ART OF CHANGE

> *Only by changing can we remain the same. And only by moving can we stay where we are.*
>
> —*Tony Buzon*

We Cannot Not Change

If there is one constant, one certainty in life, it is change. An old Zen saying says that you cannot enter the river the same way twice. Similarly, the conditions in life will be different each time, like entering a new river. The human body itself is constantly changing. Cells, blood and organs work towards change, without rest, to maintain homeostasis or perfect equilibrium. In other words, to be able to remain healthy, the body constantly changes.

It is a spontaneous mechanism that happens constantly in nature. We all have had the experience, when we have a lake, a sea, a river or a pool—and we find ourselves in water so deep that our feet don't touch the bottom. How do we maintain our position? We must move. Paradoxically, to remain where we are, we must change, remain in motion. And we must do so in a coordinated way, giving rhythm and direction to our actions.

Day after day, we are changing. But in what direction are we changing? Are we flowing with the current? Or are we sinking?

The Five Stages of Change

In his studies, about learning and change, the famous anthropologist Gregory Bateson notes five levels.

Level zero consists of resistance to change. Even if we are not satisfied with the results that we achieve, we continue to do the same things, have the same habits. By doing this, we have an illusion of stability and of safety. In reality, however, we are actually changing. But we are not changing for the better. On the contrary, the more we continue to use these methods that don't work, the more we are troubled. "As long as it's fast; I don't have time to waste." Phillip is a sales director of an important multinational company. People who work with him are afraid of his rough manners, his tension-filled silences and his authoritative ways. They refer to him as "father-master." For this reason, the CEO of the company asked us to guide him with some coaching sessions.

"It's my nature," Phillip explains, "and, besides, it's the only way to get results, to get ahead." At home, the situation is not any better. "Lately, my wife has mentioned getting a separation; my kids don't really talk with me, and my working environment is more and more hostile," he confessed—while playing with a pack of cigarettes, which he seemed to be smoking more and more often.

For years, Phillip has behaved in the same way. Lately, he has gained weight, often has headaches and is always nervous. In this case, the change is not desired because, day after day, things are getting worse. The first level of change happens when we start to learn something new which will help us do something different. We struggle to adapt, to develop flexibility and new ways to react to situations.

This level is known as "incremental change;" slowly we begin to achieve better results.

During the sessions, Phillip learned to manage his personal, family and work time. At the beginning, it was difficult, but, little by little, he gained new and healthier habits. He quit smoking, drank less alcohol and started a regular running routine, all of which made him more relaxed.

As we gradually develop new habits and confront situations differently, our point of view grows, and, before long, we realize that we have only just begun to improve and that there's a long way to go. We are in the "developmental change" phase, where we begin to develop new capacities and seek new territory.

Continuing his coaching sessions, Phillip began to understand his behavior. "I'm embarrassed to admit it, but, until now, I saw people only by their function. They were just numbers with which to generate sales, and everyone was my servant. I was the same at home: I expected that my needs came before everyone else's."

Quickly Phillip understood that there was more than managing stress that he needed to learn. "I want to learn to be more open and positive with my colleagues. I want to learn to see their worth and respect their needs. I want to learn to hug my children and express how much I love them."

Like Phillip, our change is not just in our behaviors, our work, our relationships; it is in the deepest part of us.

This is the "evolutionary" level.

Phillip discovered a new world to which he had never been before, that of emotional intelligence: tenderness, empathy, equality, and mutual support. He even found that he had an artistic side and loved to paint. When a new identity emerges, it changes our whole world, guides our choices and gives us new direction. It is the moment of "reawakening." In fact, it brings an actual revolution to our very existence.

He participated, with other members of the group, in many of our personal development classes and asked if he could be trained to become a coach. He is, at this point, actually a mentor at work, someone who is greatly respected, the one with the highest performance and motivation. What about his wife and children? After their initial disbelief, they are happy with his change: "He seems like another person. It's been a true revolution!" they told us happily.

Often it is difficult to measure change because it's not something that we can see or touch. And yet it is something concrete: it is a process that happens right before our eyes.

WHAT IS AT THE FOUNDATION OF CHANGE?

As the Bateson study concluded, the key words are "to learn" and "to grow."

We change as we grow, and, in the meantime, we learn and develop new talents, ideas and behaviors. While we incorporate our new lessons, something inside us begins to change. The beginning of change is innate in every human just like the ability to walk. No one is born knowing how to walk. The development of this ability revolutionizes our entire existence. Then, over time, if we want, we can even improve on this talent and, with training, become dancers, runners or athletes.

In the same way, we can use our natural capacity for change to make big or small daily transformations.

ACCEPTANCE

> *God, grant me the serenity to accept the things*
> *that I cannot change, the courage to change*

*the things that I can and the wisdom to know
the difference.*

—*Saint Francis*

Years ago, my husband and I wanted to create a new
version of community where we could live in the country
together with friends and colleagues, in the lap of nature.
For this, we examined many farmhouses and old abandoned
estates before finding the perfect one. After signing the lease,
with renovation plans ready and even the furniture chosen,
we found that we could not go ahead. For a variety of reasons, we had to give up the house, at least for the time being.

My first reaction was total denial of what was happening:
"No, it's not true! There are no real obstacles. I will do it!"

For months and months, I continued to try and try; the
idea of not achieving my dream was too much. But whatever
solutions I tried to find, I continued to bang my head against
a wall.

Then, all of a sudden, I got it! Maybe it was time to
accept that I could not change it. Only when I completely
realized this (and it was not easy) did I find that I did not
have to completely give up on the project as I had thought.
And that's how it was! Instead of continuing to follow the
initial dream, we redirected our search toward a simple house
in the country. All of a sudden, everything changed! In less
than a month, we found a beautiful home at a price that
we could afford. Nicola and I moved there and many of the
friends that were part of the initial project now live close by.
If we had not opened our minds to change, we would still be
living in Milan and we would still be fighting with lawyers,
surveyors, and architects.

There's an old saying that I always try to keep in mind:
if I can change something, why should I worry? And, if

it's something that I cannot change, why should I worry? Without having an open mind, determination degenerates into stubbornness, the creative tension becomes nervousness and frustration and the change becomes a war! It is only by accepting the situation that we can create the necessary conditions to increase our capacity to learn from experience and go toward evolutionary change.

But what is acceptance? And, more than that, what is it not?

Often, when I approach these discussions in my courses, I hear someone asking if, in accepting life as it comes, are we not becoming inert and mere spectators of life? If I accept every situation, won't I risk complacency and actually block any change?

Once a woman, who often came to our sessions, acknowledged she was a victim of domestic violence. She mentioned that she *accepted* the fact that she was regularly beaten by her husband. That is not an example of acceptance, but of resignation because, in that situation, things could have been changed.

The big difference is that resigning oneself to the situation is a passive state of mind. Resigning oneself is the same as accepting, often against one's will, and to become closed within our self, playing the role of the victim.

Accepting inevitable events requires strength, courage, desire and determination to go forward. It means taking note of how things are, listening to the call to change, stopping putting your head under the sand, and recognizing what is happening and being honest with yourself.

OBSERVE WITHOUT JUDGMENT: BLESSING OR BAD LUCK?

Before acceptance can occur, it's necessary to observe without judgment, with sincere curiosity. As soon as we judge, we become rigid in our position. This pollutes our capability to see the nuances; it contaminates our interpretation of the world and alters our responses to events.

An old Taoist story tells of a wise man who lived in a village in the northernmost part of China. One day his son let their best horse escape. His father, the wise man, told him, "How can you tell that it's bad luck and not a blessing?"

Months later the horse returned bringing with it a beautiful stallion. Now the boy was radiant in his good luck and the whole village congratulated him for his fortune.

But the father said, "How can you say that this is good luck and not a disaster?"

The stallion quickly became the favorite of the boy, but, one day, while in the saddle, the boy fell and broke his hip. Once again, the father said, "How can you tell that this is bad luck and not a blessing?"

A few months later a nomad tribe invaded the north of China and all the able men were drafted to combat the enemy. The boy was not due to his injury. Nine out of ten never returned home. The fall from the horse saved his life! The boy and his father lived happily taking care of each other for many years.

As this story reminds us, how can we say that what we think is bad luck is not actually a blessing? We should face reality keeping our observation as realistic as possible, being sure not to judge based on preconceived ideas.

And When I Fail?

Let's go back to the time when we learned how to walk. We all tried over and over and failed many, many times. But we never felt as though we had failed, and no one ever judged us! This allowed us to get up each and every time and to continue to try to get better every day. Oh, how different things would be if we could have the same accepting approach—with no judging—to all the failures of life!

Acceptance allows us to love ourselves and to appreciate ourselves even if our take off is not perfect—even if we fall for the hundredth time. The psychologist author Nathan Freeman suggests, "You must love and accept your psychosis before you can heal."

Is that how easy it is? No, not really. It's simple but it's not easy because there is a trap. How many times have we thought that we accepted reality when, instead, we have merely rationalized and inside we are angry, discouraged and feeling guilty? True acceptance comes only when we are open to absorbing and to completely digest what it is.

As we will see later, often it's exactly the things that we cannot change, like grief, sickness, and separations, which teach us and make the most important transformations of our lives. And often it is the most difficult situations that change us. During the courses, much of our work consists of helping people make exactly this passage.

We will look more deeply at things that will help you develop self-acceptance, such as optimism, mediation along with faith and spirituality.

If we do not accept something (a situation, an experience, a part of ourselves), how can we completely own it? And if we don't own it, how can we change it?

THE POWER ZONE

If you don't like something, change it. If you can't change it, change your attitude. Don't complain.

—Maya Angelou

"Nobody around here helps you even if you're drowning in work. I wish things were different, but what can I do!" Up until she arrived in class an hour ago, Roseanne had a forced smile on her face that was not difficult to notice. There is a big difference between the cheek muscles that worked to show her teeth—worthy of a whitening toothpaste commercial—and her deer eyes, where there was not a trace of happiness! Is this what Paul Ekman[1] would have called the "Pan Am" smile?

It happened again. I was distracted. When a person shows a strong contradiction between what he/she says and what his body expresses, I tend to follow the body clues. My attention was immediately drawn to the resigned tone with which the woman continued, "Nothing will ever change. People talk about cooperating, but, in the end, everybody worries about their own. How can one work in a place where no one even greets you in the morning?"

So I decide to try something. "Up to now, what have you done to make the situation better? How many times have you been the first to say 'hello' in the morning?"

"Oh, no, they should greet me! I have already tried enough. When we started to share the office, I greeted both Louise and Mary. They did answer me—but without even lifting their eyes from the computer screen." Rosanne was on the defensive. My experiment failed.

---

[1] Paul Ekman is a psychology professor at the University of San Francisco who studied facial expression for many years and cataloged nineteen different types of smiles distinguishing between fake ones and real ones. Ekman called real smiles "Duchenne" after a psychologist who demonstrated that the smile is a physiological response to a state of well-being, so much so that we smile from the time we are in the womb. Among the false smiles that don't involve the nerves and muscles of the cheeks and eyes, the most famous are those of Pan Am because they remind us of the fake welcoming smile of the typical airline hostess of the now bankrupt American company.

"Have you ever thought that, at that time they were very busy or maybe morning greetings were not very important to them? Have you ever spoken to them about it?" I asked, continuing to be surprised at how, in large companies, it is often the little things that affect the well-being and productivity of the workers.

"Well, we're all busy. They should come and apologize. They are ruining my life." Rosanne's tone was getting dryer and the tension in her jaws more and more visible. My second experiment failed. It was a shame that she didn't realize that it was she who was ruining her life.

I gave it one more shot. "How can Louise and Mary ruin your life? Who tells you how to react to situations? Do you want it to be others? Do you want to give these people the power, or do you want it to be yourself that decides for you and for your life?"

Silence...Rosanne did not move for a few seconds. Then suddenly her jaws relaxed. No, wait, I think they actually dropped! "Of course not! No one can ruin our day or our life unless we give them permission. I never looked at the situation from that point of view," she responded with one of the best expressions of surprise that I have ever seen. This time it worked. It's such a simple concept; why do we continually forget it?

THE TWO ZONES

There are two very clear areas in which we move. One is a zone of which we are completely in control and another which is completely foreign to us and which we cannot influence. How often we wish we could have everything under our control: the behavior of our partner, the choices of our children, corporate politics, traffic, and so on. And how much of all of that is actually under our control? And, even more, how much time and energy do we waste worrying, complaining and trying to change things without ever succeeding?

No one can make us feel inferior, sad or angry if we don't want them to. Nothing and no one can ruin our life if we don't allow them to. Viktor Frankl, a Viennese neuro-psychiatrist of Hebrew descent and father of logo therapy, reflecting on his long imprisonment in Auschwitz, said that whatever his jailers did to him, they could not force him to hate them and he concluded that, "…in the end, it is possible to take everything from us except one thing: the ability to choose how to act when faced with any possible circumstance." Thinking, feeling, talking and reacting are our four principal capabilities, and, together, they form our power zone. It is here that lives our engine of change.

THE CARDS OF LIFE

Mata Amritanandamayi, known all over the world as Amma, or actually Mother, is an Indian guru considered by many to be a saint because of her incredible humanitarian efforts and her precious teachings. Born in a very poor area of Kerala, she dedicated her life to alleviating the suffering of the neediest. Owning nothing but her *sari*, she was able to build many schools, orphanages and hospitals and donated more than 25,000 houses to the homeless. Her organization provides over 50,000 meals a day to the hungry. She has received many international awards and has often been invited to the United Nations. Yet, she is one of the humblest people that I have ever met. During a visit to her *ashram* in India, I heard her use a suggestive metaphor to explain our power zone. Amma compared life to a game of cards. The cards are dealt by the dealer and can be given many names: God, destiny, karma, chance, etc. Sometimes we get beautiful cards making it easy to play; at other times we get really bad cards. In each case, we have no power in choosing the cards. That which we have complete control over, however, is the way in which we play the cards. And this makes the difference in our life and the world. Having this distinction clear allows us to stop wasting time and energy trying to change things that we cannot. These are the cards that life is dealing. But, we can decide how to use them. Surely, we can choose to not care, to complain and to pass whole days being angry with the dealer of our cards. But will that make us use our cards better?

RESPONS-ABILITY

> *To live means to accept the responsibility of finding the correct answers to the problems of life.*
>
> —*Viktor Frankl*

If only I had enough money/time/good luck. If only I got more help from colleagues/family members/friends.

If only my husband supported me.

If only I were younger/thinner/prettier. If only my work was less stressful.

Does this sound familiar? What feelings and actions come to mind with this train of thought? When we find ourselves thinking and talking this way, are we in our power zone?

The line that identifies our power zone is clearly defined and has a name: *respons-ability*.

Responsibility does not mean blame. It is certainly not our fault if we were fired, left by our partner. To be responsible means to regain the ability to respond to the events. It means to be able to give the best answers to the questions that life's problems ask us. We are totally responsible for our power zone, the way we think, feel, talk and act. We are also responsible for our behavior, what we say and how we act toward others.

But we are not responsible for what others think, do or say. That is part of the other person's power zone. We can only change how we feel toward them. Understanding this mechanism will help us create relationships that are healthier, more open, more honest and more efficient.

"There are ten of us working on this floor, and there are two bathrooms. Last week the cleaning people were on leave and the bathrooms were not cleaned the whole time. Is it possible that no one could take the initiative and clean the bathroom?

"Every time that something unpleasant must be taken care of, the issue bounces from desk to desk like a hot potato and no one wants to take the responsibility. Why should I do it?

"The planet is polluted every day. Many animals are mistreated. Somebody should do something!"

EVERYONE, SOMEONE, ANYONE AND NO ONE

This is the story of four people named Everyone, Someone, Anyone and No one. There was an important job to do and Everyone was asked to do it. Everyone was sure that Someone would take care of it. Anyone could have done it, but No one did it. Someone got angry because it was Everyone's job. Everyone thought that Anyone could do it, but No one understood that Everyone would not do it. In the end, everyone blamed Someone for not doing it when No one did what Anyone could do.

This is the story of every one of us.

When faced with a difficult task, starting an uncomfortable conversation, a difficult step to take, a difficult situation to change, No one is happy. It would be much easier for Anyone to play the role of the victim and become depressed or blame others. Someone, however, uses his power zone and decides not to do it.

Every time that we choose respons-ability, we take a step forward toward evolutionary change.

TAKE POWER AWAY FROM EXTERNAL EVENTS

"So the anxiety, anger and malaise that I have felt for months were not caused by my colleagues, my husband or any external events but by my reaction to their behaviors?" Rosanne asked me this question during our lunch break, taking me aside as if she were telling a big secret. I looked at her; now her eyes were smiling. I knew that she knew the answer to the question. Relationships, in which people are responsible, are not guided by need, by control, or by expectations that are invariably disappointed. They are guided by the desire to play the game, to speak honestly and openly, by the pleasure of sharing, exchanging, from mutual understanding and respect.

It may seem that our power zone is very limited. In reality, if we use it completely, we will find that it's not at all like that. Here we meet another contrast of change: the tighter the power zone, the larger its influence.

Often we err in thinking that others have something that is not right, that they are wrong, that they are incapable of resolving problems. And, in that case, we feel as though we have to do it for them. To be aware of your own area of influence means leaving the possibility and the space for those around you to be responsible of their own thoughts, words, actions and states of mind. And this means believing in others, in their complete ability to change.

In this sense, by changing ourselves, we open the way for change even for others who desire it. When we speak of change from now on, we will take as fact that it does not mean changing others but learning how to manage ourselves better, our moods, our time, our resources and our potential. And it is from this point of view that we face change.

In the days to come, at home, at work, simply notice if and when you find yourself outside your power zone. What happened? To what or to whom did you give permission to manage your mood and your reactions?

By continuing to do that, will you live better?

IT'S MINE!

Think of something for which you feel a great sense of ownership, something that is absolutely yours and that you would not give up for anything—something about which you could say, "It's mine," with every cell in your body.

Is it your wallet? The keys to your house? Your dog? Would you give all of this up to the first person you met on the street? For what reason would you never do it? Because it's yours!

In the same way, our power zone is ours, a birthright.

Why do we give it up so easily?

PLAYING WITH THREE STRINGS

There is no passion in playing small, accepting less than what we are capable of.

—*Nelson Mandela*

It was 18 November 1995, and Itzhak Perlman, world-renowned violinist, was playing at the Lincoln Center in New York.

He had polio as a child, he had to wear braces on his legs, and he walked with difficulty even with the help of his crutches.

Anyone who had seen one of his concerts knew it.

Perlman walked across the stage very slowly. The audience waited patiently.

Finally, he sat down, put his crutches on the floor, took off his braces, and got into his characteristic pose with one foot behind the other; he bent to get the violin, placed it under his chin and made a sign to the orchestra conductor and began to play. The audience was used to this ritual.

But this time it was different. Something went wrong. After playing for a few minutes, one of the strings on his violin broke. The audience clearly heard it as if it were the shot of a gun. There was no doubt as to what Perlman would have to do.

The people thought: now he will put down the violin, put the braces back, get the crutches, head backstage, get it fixed, come back and repeat.

But he did not.

Instead, he closed his eyes for a moment, and then signaled the conductor and restarted from where he had left off. He played with such passion, purity and power that had never before been heard.

The public was enthralled.

Everyone knows that it is impossible to play a symphonic piece with only three strings.

I know it, and you know it, but that night Itzhak Perlman refused to know it. And he could be seen modifying, changing, taking apart and recomposing the symphonic piece in his mind. At a certain point, it seemed as if he played chords that were never played before. When he finished, there was a reverential silence, and then every person, in every corner of the theatre, stood, shouting and applauding to express his/her admiration.

He smiled, wiped the sweat from his brow, raised his bow to quieten them, and then said humbly, as if thinking out loud: "You know, sometimes it's the artist's job to discover how much more music he can create with what he has left."[2]

Our existence is made of difficult times also. It's made of joys and sorrows, of light and dark. Sometimes we have all four strings available, and sometimes one of the strings breaks. How do we react then?

Are we capable of accepting that a sickness forces us to be bedridden? Are we capable in those instances to keep our power zone, choose respons-ability or direct our thoughts, emotions, state of mind and behavior toward evolutionary change?

READY TO JUMP?

> *Progress is impossible without change. And those who cannot change their own mind will not be able to change anything.*
>
> *—George Bernard Shaw*

In his book *Embracing Change,* Tony Buzan, an English psychologist and intellectual, uses a very fitting example to explain human behavior when faced with change. If a frog is put in a pan of cold water and the water is quickly heated, the frog feels the sudden change, quickly notices the danger and immediately jumps out. But, if the water is heated gradually, the frog will not notice the change and, bit-by-bit, it will fall asleep and be boiled alive. In these cases, extreme adaptability, which is usually a positive quality, becomes counterproductive.

During our lives, changes come often. It is up to us to be aware of which direction life is taking us and to remember

---

[2] From an article in the *Houston Chronicle* of November 18, 1995.

the subtle, but fundamental, difference between acceptance and resignation.

THE COMFORT ZONE

We humans tend to live inside a certain safe zone, which we can define as our territory, made up of known elements: convictions, friends, family, work and sports. We are creatures of habit. Every day we tend to repeat, more or less, the same thoughts and actions as the day before.

Think about when you sit at the table with your family. What seat do you take? Do you change it often, or do you keep the same seat for years? This becomes our world, our comfort zone. All these habits make us feel safe and comfortable. There is nothing wrong with this, as long as the habits that we have created keep us continually improving and headed toward evolutionary change. But what happens, as in the cases of Phillip or Rosanne, when it's not like that?

During the reading of this book, and especially in the practical parts, you will be invited many times to leave your comfort zone. Every time, you face new ways of thinking, ways that are not part of your beliefs, or do exercises that push you to do some soul-searching, you are leaving your comfort zone. In doing this, you begin to give new direction to your life.

THE FOCUSED INTENTION

Since I really like to use the most recent scientific research of the human psyche along with time proven wisdom and philosophies, in some of my courses, we suggest a ritual that has been practice for centuries in the whole world: fire walking.

I have never liked the macho aspect that some movements have given this ancient practice. In my opinion, it's like changing something sacred into a kind of bungee jumping; it diminishes it and completely distorts its meaning. For me, the amazing thing is that fire-walking is a perfect metaphor for life.

For example, after having guided thousands of people across hot coals, I could not help but notice the significant difference between someone who unintentionally finds himself walking across fire and burns himself and a fire-walker. For centuries, all over the world, the fire-walker does not walk across the fire unintentionally; he intends to do it and has learned to focus.

Even critics of fire walking, who have walked across coals with no practice, to demonstrate that it is not possible to be burnt, have exploited the power of intended focalization to prove their point.

Occasionally, I have crossed the coals without really wanting to, distracted, almost against my will. And when I did that, I got burned every time. It's the very same that happens in life!

If we go through life without paying attention, distractedly, doing things that we don't want to do, without focusing or being driven by strong desires, it's probable that we will get burned or lulled into not realizing that it's time to jump, like the frog in the story.

Bit by bit, it all becomes a habit so well established that it is difficult for us to realize what is actually happening. The only difference is that, with fire-walking, the burn is immediate and evident, while in life, the burns are often unnoticeable, almost invisible, and seemingly acceptable. When this happens, what do we do? Instead of listening to the messages that our body is sending, we ingeniously find thousands of ways to ignore and suffocate every symptom, and we continue to tell ourselves daily that, maybe, someday, we will find the time or the way to make those changes that we know are necessary to finally live the way we want to. But, not now; we're too busy doing other things.

In the meantime, the water continues to burn us. Are you ready to jump?

THE CRUX OF THE SITUATION

> *Real discovery is not searching for new lands but looking with new eyes.*
>
> —*Marcel Proust*

Where Are We Searching?

A traveler walks past the home of an elderly woman kneeling in her garden. The man stops and asks what she is doing. She answers that she has lost her precious earrings and is looking for them. The traveler then offers to help her, but, after many hours of sifting through the garden, they find nothing. The man then asks exactly where she lost them, and the woman answers that she lost them in the bedroom. Startled, the traveler asks why is she searching in the garden, and the woman responds—almost annoyed, "It's obvious! The bedroom is dark, and I'd never find them there; at least I can see in the garden."

This is the same thing that we do when we try to find answers that are not familiar to us. How can we hope to find answers that are outside our control, far away from our comfort zone?

Taking stock of the situation means beginning to look within ourselves, even if it means that we must explore dark places. It means accepting reality, understanding what is within our power zone and what is not, and taking responsibility for the answers that we give by means of our thoughts, emotions, words and actions.

Sharpening Your Tools

Stephen Covey, in his bestseller, *The 7 Habits of Highly Effective People,* tells a story that fascinated me and I have used often in my classes.

Once there was a young woodcutter whose dream was to become the greatest woodcutter of all time. He worked very hard and had little time for all the rest—friends, family and his girlfriend. One day he was in the woods, cutting, when an elderly stranger came toward him. The old man, who was feeble and thin, weak on his legs and had a long white beard, smiled at him and said, "Young man, come and sit with me; I have something to tell you."

But the boy did not have time; he had other things to do and began to get agitated.

The old man remained silent and thought. Then his face lit up. "I have an idea," he said. "I dare you. On Sunday, from dawn to sunset, we will see who can cut the most wood—me or you!"

The young man looked at him, not believing his ears. Just by looking at their builds and considering their age difference, he was sure that he would win. He accepted the challenge. The whole town would be there watching, and it would be a great opportunity for him.

Finally, Sunday arrived and the race began. The young man did not stop for a second and worked with all the strength he had. The old man cut wood, but every once in a while, he sat down. When the sun started to set, the mayor called the end of the contest, and the two piles were weighed.

Incredibly, the wood cut by the old man weighed much more than the boy's. The boy was stunned. Incredulous, he went to the old man and angrily asked, "How is this possible? I did not stop all day long but you did stop and sat down more than once. What trick did you use?"

The old man looked at him, and, with the same calm smile as he had during their first meeting, answered, "Young man, that's what I was trying to tell you in the woods the other day, but you did not have time to listen. It's true. I sat down every once in a while, but when I stopped, I was actually sharpening my tools."

To take stock of the situation means to stop a bit and use the time to sharpen our tools.

It means to be honest and ask ourselves where we are, where we are headed, where we would rather be, and what stops us from getting there, what tools could we use to make it happen and what direction should we go in.

CHAPTER 2

WHERE ARE WE?

It is at the outside that we search for causes and solutions to all the problems of the world. In our haste, we forget the greatest truth: the foundation of all problems is in the mind of man. We forget that the world cannot become good if the individual minds do not become good.

—*Mata Arritanandamayi*

As we have seen, evolutionary change is not a magic pill that we can take one evening and see the effects the next morning; it is an endless voyage.

As in all natural processes, this voyage requires time and patience, and the result goes way beyond the finish line. In fact, the map itself will change. We will change bit by bit as we travel along the path of knowledge.

At what point are you in your personal voyage? What are you doing to spur change? This is a process that will last your whole life, and, perhaps, even beyond, but it is exactly because of this that it is so exciting. Every day will bring new challenges and new goals.

Who would want, once headed for an exciting destination, to finish the trip the fastest possible and to hurry back home? Once you have begun your journey toward conscious evolution, you will never go back. It's like living in an enormous house and realizing that you have been staying in the kitchen only. Once you realize your potential, would you choose to go backward?

Some east African populations have a beautiful song that says something like this: "I decided to follow the road of the fire of knowledge; there is no return, there is no return."

I have personal experience.

THE CALL

It's not so important what we expect from life as what life expects from us.

—*Viktor Frankl*

During my childhood, I lived in Africa between Zambia, Tanzania and Nigeria. It was at the end of the sixties and these nations had just achieved their independence from the British government. Zambia and Tanzania became independent in 1964, the year I was born. In a way, these African nations and I are the same age and have grown up together. Like me, during my adolescence, they, young and lively too, experimented with liberty.

The colonial system hadn't worked very well at unifying the single nations, preparing them for independence. Nigeria was hit especially hard with ethnic conflicts, each group with its own needs and quest for power and supremacy over the others.

During those years, we often witnessed fights, guerrillas and bloody riots. If I look back on my life now, I have the definite sensation, as do many people that every part of our life, beginning at childhood, exists to prepare us for the journey that we will take in the future.

I cannot, of course, say that I consciously chose the experience of Africa, but I can undoubtedly see that all of it—even the parts that were not easy—was the perfect training for what would happen later.

But, while it was happening, I was not aware.

Only now can I see, clearly, how those turbulent years were the best training for learning how to go through turbulent times in human nature.

What Nigeria was going through then, was, in fact, not very different from what happens to the human soul during moments of crisis, when we harden our hearts while trying to manage the various parts that live within us. My father chose to live in those places. It couldn't have been easy for him to make that decision. It took him away from everything and everybody, but, as often happens at crossroads in life, when he chose this path, an offer for a job that was to last only a few months—but lasted thirty years—changed his life and ours, and it made him a new man.

I was not much over ten years old when my father was diagnosed with a strain of malaria that was considered incurable by traditional medicine. There were no doctors in the area, and, even if there had been, I'm not sure if my father would have contacted them. He had been in Africa for too long, and, just like the colors of the sunsets and the aromas of that land enter your blood, your beliefs and convictions begin to mesh with the ancient traditions of the place.

Encouraged by the advice of Alyu, a friend and colleague of my father, we consulted the shaman of his village. After a few days, the old shaman, who could barely speak English,

solemnly entered our home. I watched curiously and carefully as he opened the bag and, while saying incomprehen-
sible words, took out the tail of a monkey. He made gestures around my father, who was shaking with fever. Then
he offered it to my father and told him to put in under his
pillow and sleep. The malaria would go away.

The next morning when I woke up, I found my father
in the kitchen, whistling and full of energy, with no sign of
weakness from the sickness of the past days. Despite the general disbelief of the family and many friends, my father never
again suffered from malaria attacks. We were so amazed by
this cure that we never talked about it. We could not make
sense of what happened, but I think it was in that moment
that I decided, at least consciously, that I would build myself
in that place. I would dedicate my life to exploring the capacities of human beings, their hidden potential and the elements that make up this capacity.

However, what seemed so possible and reachable in
Africa, with the local beliefs, seemed to disappear and
become a faint memory once I returned to Italy. My attention went to my friends, the current fashion trends and my
first high-heeled shoes.

For all my high school years, I continued to read inspirational books and listen to the Beatles and the Inti Illimani.
My heroes were Mahatma Gandhi, Martin Luther King, and
Che Guevara. I dreamed of revolution, but I didn't realize
that the revolution that I needed was within myself.

As soon as I finished high school, fascinated by the idea
of becoming economically independent and having a job
that left time for studying as well, I became a model. In those
days of the 1980s, there was no competition like today; models weren't famous like rock stars. But fashion was becoming very important, and, if you had a decent body and some

intelligence, you could make a career, travel the world and make good money.

For ten years, I was completely immersed in that world of fashion shows, photography shoots and casting, almost forgetting the promise I had made to myself as a child.

But my destiny was apparently always there and, in quiet moments, when there were fewer external stimuli, they appeared as a kind of anxiety.

I travelled a lot and tried to quiet this existential distress with everything I had: work, relationships, clothes, vacations, food, cigarettes and daily life. For a little more than a year, this seemed to work.

I didn't understand yet, but the pleasure that I found in travelling was just a push toward travelling within myself. What needed to improve was my internal world. Instead, I was very busy exploring the external one. And there was a reason for it. An interior change would be painful, would mean discussing my identity, my whole life. It would mean completely leaving my comfort zone. I had everything imaginable but my anxiety would not go away. The only choice I had was to pay attention to it, accept it and take responsibility for it. But it wasn't easy. I read more, began to meditate regularly and participated in meetings and seminars on personal growth. During my frequent travelling for work, I used every opportunity to contact the local native populations of every place I went, so much so that I decided to stay in certain places, like the Far East and Central America for months.

In the silence, I discovered parts of myself that I didn't know about until then—fears, hopes, thoughts and dreams that I had denied for years. All of this transformed me bit by bit. Even my body felt different in a thousand small ways. For example, after having gone for months without shoes, it was difficult to put on any type of footwear. You can imagine how I felt at the fashion shows when I had to wear sandals with at least five inch heels. I tried to recreate peaceful moments backstage to do some meditation, despite the chaos; some of my colleagues accompanied me. Can you just imagine three models sitting in the lotus position in the space between the clothing racks while chanting a loud "om"?

I gradually lost interest in the things that used to be important to me: clothes, chic locales, even my own physical appearance. To the people around me, the change was very evident and, for many, quite worrisome. The journey toward transformation had begun. My life was no longer the same. Just like the soil that must be aerated before being reseeded, every bit of my person had to dissolve before I could enjoy a new life. This internal revolution involved my whole life— from my marriage to my work.

The one, who was married a few years earlier, was the old Lucia, with the old beliefs and values. Now I was completely changed. The man I had married was a beautiful person and I loved him. But inside I knew that this threshold had to be crossed alone and that our paths were not going in the same direction. We had travelled for a while in the same train, and it had been very nice, but now I was called to get off and travel alone. To tell the truth, that sounded like a torturous and difficult path that wound through the chasms of steep mountains. I didn't even know if there would be a refuge at the top where I could rest. But I couldn't, nor did I want to, go back. It was as if the journey possessed me.

My work lost meaning and didn't represent what I was now; I didn't want to live my life like that. I decided to abandon the fashion world.

My mother, with great pride, told me, since I was little, that I had my head on my shoulders. In that moment, I suspected that it was somewhere else.

When I had started that work, I knew that I couldn't be a model forever, and, seeing that I had my head on my shoulders, shortly after, I started a studio that organized fashions shows, a modeling agency and a school for models. That was going to be my future. Thanks to my hard work and that of my three partners, the business was going very well. Nonetheless, when I left to take classes in psychology and various techniques for personal growth, I asked myself if I was losing my mind. I wanted to explore human potentiality, learn how to use it better, live a significant full life and give classes to help others do the same. The problem was that I didn't have the certainty that I could make it. I had to build it day by day, fighting with inner demons that told me that I would never be good enough. A few months later, a friend who was in charge of his company's training, asked if I wanted to be his assistant at a seminar on self-esteem and the development of talents in Assisi, Italy. Seeing that I had long studied this topic and had participated in many of these groups, I thought that maybe, at the end of the day, I could actually give my opinion and suggest some new ideas.

I decided to accept.

So, I met my friend George in Florence and we travelled together to Assisi the night before the course was to begin.

A few hours after we arrived at the hotel, George called me to his room. "I'm terribly sick; my fever is 104 and my throat is burning. There's no way I can conduct the class tomorrow; can you do it for me?" he weakly asked.

"Are you crazy? Don't even think about it!" was my first response.

But, after a while, I realized that the participants were already there and to refuse would be an insult to my friend, the participants and, especially, to myself.

I think I spent the night awake and changed my mind at least a hundred times, but, when the sun rose, I had made up my mind. I would take the class. So, with shaking legs and voice, I entered the classroom at nine in the morning.

Despite my fears, the seminar was great. Some months later, the same agency asked me to do another. I could do it. That could be my new occupation and a fundamental part of my new life. Thus, the reconstruction period began.

Obviously, internal journeys don't always cause such radical changes, but when we begin to think and act differently, the transformation will knock on our door. And it will do everything until we open it.

PLEASURE AND HAPPINESS

> *Like those who ignore where a treasure is hidden walking by it, over and over, without discovering it, so do all creatures, as if immersed in sleep, live every day without finding the world of Brahman, distracted, that they are, by nonessentials.*

—Chandogya Upanishad 8.3.2

Often change means giving up a sense of security. Even a relationship that has dragged on for years or a job that we aren't passionate about but that gives us financial security are things that have become habits and make us feel safe.

Before becoming courageous enough to leave our comfort zone and confront all of this, we must be able to notice the signs that show us that we need change. But how are those signs recognized?

RECOGNIZING THE SIGNS

If you take my example, the first sign was a slight discontent. Even though my life seemed perfect, I wasn't satisfied. To make me feel alive, I needed many emotions, most of which came from external sources, such as social events, relationships, job satisfaction, trips, new clothes…Amma, whom I met many years later, would have said that I was behaving like a child who is crying because he is hungry. He needs milk, but when he finds a pacifier, he calms down. For a while, it works, but, before long, he becomes tired of the pacifier, which certainly cannot satisfy his hunger.

From the outside, my life may have seemed satisfying but the rewards were fewer and lasting less; my days weren't spent building values in my life, helping me to grow, or making me a better person. This is why my dissatisfaction kept creeping back. But what was the key? Looking back, I now see that for years I confused pleasure with happiness. I can clearly understand how my frantic search for the first prohibited me from finding the second. I ask myself how many other people are still confusing the two ideas.

True happiness, as we will see in the section dedicated to where we want to go, is what makes our lives worthwhile and when we are moving toward evolutionary change. Happiness is found by doing the right things, by making investments that allow us to accumulate emotional and mental wealth helping us to grow, to develop quality, to find new talents and to build our life the way we want to.

Pleasure has other characteristics. In his book *The Construction of Happiness,* Martin Seligman, professor of psychology at the University of Pennsylvania and ex-president of the American Psychological Association, explains that when we taste pleasure we are consuming something, while happiness implies making investments of time, money, or energy—with the promise of a long-term reward for ourselves and/or for others.

We come across this kind of choice every day—even in the simplest of things. When we get home from work, do we invest our time in reading a stimulating book or do we sink in front of the TV? At the moment, the choice of TV is certainly the easiest—uses the least energy and the fewest movements. But, in the long run, which choice will give the most reward?

Think about the things that are usually thought of as the pleasures of life: good food, good wine, good sex—all, if possible, in front of a fireplace or a beautiful panorama. They are immediate pleasures that are felt through the five senses and involve the body. And they are immediate, but, despite the fact that they probably induce positive feelings, the feelings dissolve very quickly once the stimulus disappears.

They also produce addiction. In fact, only the first sips of your favorite brandy, the first bites of chocolate or the first rays of sun on your skin give that shiver of intense pleasure. Try to keep eating the chocolate, drinking the brandy or staying in the sun for a whole day and you'll quickly realize that the sensation is not so satisfying after all. The fifth or sixth bite of chocolate give a less intense pleasure than the first, and, after a while, the taste is gone; all that's left are the calories. It's not much different with sex.

Unless you spread these pleasures over time, their silly effect actually ends up becoming nauseating. This process has a neurological reason. The neurons, the cells that make up the brains, are programmed to respond in a particularly intense way to new stimuli because they give new information. In fact, there is a short lapse of time, known as the refractory period, in which single neurons do not even respond if the stimulus is known.

I've always asked myself if this is why we're always looking for new pleasures, tastes, loves, and adventures. Maybe to run from the addiction, we search for experiences so our neurons will make us feel the shivers of emotion. Often we get lost in this research!

Not only does this type of pleasure fade quickly, but it brings risk as well.

ADDICTED TO PLEASURE?

About forty years ago, a group of scientists discovered pleasure centers in rat brains. The researchers had inserted wires in the area under the cerebral cortex, and, every time the rats pushed a certain lever, they received a pleasant stimulation via an electric shock. Very quickly, the rodents began to prefer that electric stimulation to anything else, including food and sex, and didn't do anything else but push that lever all day long. The scientists discovered the basis of habituation. It was the stimulation itself that caused the need. So if the need was satisfied by the stimulation, the next stimulation generated a strong need all over again. And so on! If the rats had stopped pushing the bar in search of the electric shock of pleasure, they would have diminished the impelling need. But they didn't.

We are used to associating the idea of addiction to heavy drugs. However, addiction extends to a much larger area. All of us have our pleasure lever, and, as soon as we can, we run to push it so that we can get the stimulation. There's nothing wrong with this as long as it doesn't become a way to numb ourselves, to cope, and, like the boiling water for the frogs, give up and avoid the call of change.

In this way the search for pleasure becomes an obstacle to change and true happiness, as we will soon see.

LET'S BE QUIET

> *Life is what happens to us while we are busy with other projects.*
>
> —*Anthony De Mello*

Faster and Faster

Most of the technological discoveries of the last century, from the airplane to the telephone to the internet, helped us to do more and to do it all faster. It has opened huge possibilities to exchange information and has made communication possible with people in far off places improving our work and our lives, but it has become a luxury to take the time to sharpen our own tools and to take stock of the situation.

Simplifying and taking shortcuts sometimes allows us to better use our time and to reach our goals more quickly. The problem begins when we use these ways indiscriminately in every situation without even realizing it, and we aren't even aware of the effects that it has on our lives.

SHORTCUTS TO HAPPINESS

Modern civilization offers more and more of what Seligman defines, in his earlier cited book, as shortcuts to happiness: television, alcohol, drugs, shopping, paid sex, soccer games and fast food to name only a few.

To distance ourselves from these temptations while searching for true happiness is particularly difficult. It requires great effort, something that, while living in our comfort zone, we are not used to.

But what happens if we wait and spend our lives this way, with easy pleasures, never having to try too hard? The answer is worrisome: it is the way to depression. One of the main characteristics of depression is, in fact, a total concentration on one's self and on one's lack of well-being. The sensation of pleasure, as we have seen first-hand, is, by nature, elusive and makes our expectations unachievable. Being accustomed to the fast life, we are becoming impatient. This is the path to discontent.

What do we do when we begin to feel discontent? Instead of recognizing the sign and asking ourselves what to change, how to learn something new or how to adjust our aim to make our life better, we dive into some new pleasure to anesthetize ourselves and numb the symptom. And if we don't do that, we use shortcuts to fill our days so we won't have time to think about it, to feel it or to react to it.

We leave the house with our iPod earphones and throw ourselves into the traffic; we're on the phone or in front of the computer for the whole day. If we work with people, we are often distracted, pushed to hurry and by the temptation to do a thousand things at a time. Then we go home exhausted to fall on the couch in front of the TV where the role models we are fed are those of publicity, sitcoms or movies. Faced with beautiful families, perfect and smiling, we end up losing the battle and feeling completely inadequate.

So we go shopping because, thanks to the thousands of products that we can buy, we will finally feel great and seem a little bit more like our TV idols. It doesn't matter how much we spend. We agree to buy more so we can pay in installments even up to 2090.

Of course, there are some who also have a social life. Dinners, cocktails, fashionable locales to show off our latest purchases—the designer dress, the luxury watch, the new car, the chrome bike or the beautiful house. In this way, our life is filled with many social engagements where, in general, everybody talks and nobody listens. Most of the time, the music is so loud that, even if you wanted to, you would find it impossible to hear each other.

All this is nothing more than a mirror of human life. The noise of our existence makes us deaf, incapable of listening to the real calls of life, incapable of understanding from which direction they are coming.

We live a perpetual and stressful race against time in order to get us the results that we want. Even if we are able to have a rich full life from a material standpoint, we are often still incapable of being as happy and satisfied as we wish.

Often we exchange simple patches for real solutions to our problems. It's like trying to fix a broken leg with a Band-Aid. When our life doesn't work, we think that a new dress, a new love, a pill, a cigarette or a good wine will be the solution. Without realizing, we are behaving like those lab rats that continually press the lever to get the pleasurable sensation. But for how long can we do this? And, moreover, where will all of this take us?

We are doing no more than triggering a downward spiral toward involution, that which Bateson called the change of zero degrees.

EMPTINESS

What is the meaning of life? Why are we on earth? These were questions that I asked my maternal grandmother and other relatives constantly, ending up with asking even friends and my parents. People came close and said, "Hello, pretty one," and, expecting a little smile, were bombarded with million-dollar questions. No wonder, I was eventually told that it would be better not to ask certain questions. I think that was the part of me that, thirty years later, together with the long and frequent visits to so-called third world countries, still needed to know and pushed me to silence and to stop using "anesthetics" that society offered.

I still don't have certain and definitive answers to what the meaning of life is, but I definitely know that it's not palliative. At a certain point in my life, all this noise became absurd. Filling my life with mundane things no longer made sense. And, that is how, very slowly, I encountered emptiness.

According to the teachings of many current mystics, it is only in this state of internal silence that we can contact our truth and our soul. I had no other choice but to live in this vacuum.

I accepted it, thus, preventing my paralysis. I learned to recognize my fears, my frustrations and my many fictitious needs.

From here emerged clear knowledge that I was betraying a commitment to myself, the one taken after the episode with the African shaman and I wasn't following my true dreams, the ones that life had prepared me for.

This knowledge triggered the transformation process. In the section dedicated to the stages of change, you'll have the opportunity to ask yourself some of the same questions that I asked myself during this process and that helped me cross this bridge.

If we honestly want to take stock of the situation, the first step is to stop compulsively pushing the pleasure lever and, instead, create moments of silence. We must be ready to face what emerges and accept it.

It takes a lot of courage, but it's the only way to truly know ourselves.

CRISIS OR OPPORTUNITY

> *When our heart cries for things lost, our soul is happy for what is found.*
>
> —*Old Sufi proverb*

The Initiation

In tribal societies, adolescents are taught by the elders. This knowledge helps them overcome challenges, develop talents, temper their will and form their new adult personality. Once this phase is over, they are ready for a true and real initiation, a series of trials, often very difficult and physically painful. In certain tribes, it culminates in cuts that leave large scars, which remain visible for the rest of their lives. These are symbols of the capacity and the force acquired. Every time a member of the tribe, or the initiate himself, sees those scars, they are reminded of their capacity to overcome difficulty.

In our society, there is no such rite. We live years accumulating ideas of all kinds of material without learning to know ourselves. Once an adolescent, when we begin to feel the fire of life burn within, we don't have the means or the necessary moral strength to manage it. Our priests of the rite of passage into adulthood are television and publicity; the examples offered are sports and movie idols. We end up comparing ourselves to false models and having false ideals. We live in a fictitious world, and, like sleepwalkers, leave the interior flame, untended, to burn our lives.

At a certain point, life itself provides us with the trials but we have no preparation. Most of the time, we don't even have a tribe around to support us. If we don't listen to the signs of change and life itself, life will call us to change anyway, often taking away some of our security and pushing us out of our comfort zone.

As an adolescent, I thought that the initiation rituals of certain African tribes seemed barbaric and cruel, but now, after many years and many experiments, I automatically compare their cutting and scars with the inevitable pains that existence leaves in our hearts.

A sickness, the loss of someone dear, the end of a marriage or friendship, a big sentimental disappointment, being fired from a job, a failure: these all leave scars, albeit internal, that even Malidoma Patrice Somé sustains in his book, *The Healing Wisdom of Africa*. Because these initiations arrive without warning or preparation, and, because we often have no strategy to avoid the pain or deny it, we try to not think about it and to anesthetize ourselves with all our power.

This can all be helpful in the acute phase, when the wound is very recent, but, as with the tribal initiations, the trials are there to help us develop our potential and to push us toward the next stage of life. To be able to wake up, you first have to realize that you're sleeping.

As happens to the fire when we forge metal, often, only after passing through the flame of suffering and completely feeling it, are we ready to open our eyes and look within. Sometimes it is only in those moments that we are able to say, "Enough!" Finally, we perceive a sense of urgency that brings us out of immobility or away from our multiple distractions and gets us moving.

Anthropologist Michael Meade addresses the idea: "Initiation events signal forever the life of a man or a woman and pushes them to enter more deeply into their lives than they ever would have…. It is that which defines the identity of an individual or allows them to escape from prison or what takes away everything until there's nothing left but himself."

At the End of Suffering

Viktor Frankl, while analyzing his long experience in the concentration camps, sustains that, by observing the behavior of his companions, one could easily tell who had a good chance of surviving and who did not.

"Those people (the ones who would not make it)," tells Frankl in his autobiography *In Search of a Meaning of Life,* "are those who forgot that, often, it's only an external situation so terribly difficult that gives human beings the possibility to grow spiritually and beyond oneself. Instead of taking the difficulty of the concentration camp as a test of one's inner strength, they preferred to close their eyes and live in the past… and their life lost every meaning. In reality, there was a great opportunity and challenge. One could transform that experience into a victory and make it become an interior triumph in their life—or they could ignore the challenge and simply vegetate, as many of the prisoners did."

Frankl also introduced an interesting theory about the significance of suffering that closely resembles the concept of initiation. The Viennese psychiatrist believed that when we don't know what the outcome will be—the higher reason—the suffering becomes interminable and we are overwhelmed by it.

In the moment, however, in which we accept it and are ready to see the new possibilities that are being offered, we begin to tame it. We realize that we support it better and we actually find it useful. Knowing that there actually is an end to it allows us to welcome the suffering gives us courage to confront it and helps us to end it on our own.

This is the same mechanism that is the basis of training for sports, especially competitive ones. Athletes would not be able to achieve any results if they were not ready to go through a phase of suffering. Think about the hours that are spent training in all kinds of weather conditions to the limits of physical exhaustion. Diana Bianchedi, the woman's fencing champion in Atlanta in 1996, who, with broken tendons, finished the race on only one foot and arrived 15 to 7 against the Chinese Wang. Just think of the pain she had! Is that the way we stop our pain, be it physical or emotional?

Such an understanding of pain allows us to escape the infantile idea that painful experience is, in and of itself, negative.

The way in which we respond to suffering determines if it will become, for us, a way to strengthen our emotional mental muscles or if it will become merely a crutch for inertia and inactivity.

It is interesting to note that the definition of the word crisis in Chinese is the same as the definition of the word chance. In effect, the situation of crisis allows us to break the false equilibrium and open space to create new and more functional ones.

If we want this to be true for us also, the first step is to have the courage to feel pain, frustration and dissatisfaction, to face fear and to consider the scars of the initiation.

What Else Can We Do?

The genius is not the one who answers the question, but the one who asks the questions.

—Anonymous

Often we give up on the idea of following our dreams because we think that we don't possess the necessary qualities. We are convinced that, as simple human beings, we cannot do any more when all we need to do is simply look around to have continuous examples of the exact opposite. History is filled with thousands of men and women who not only made real and true miracles, but also influenced the destiny of humanity.

In the last few years, while guiding the rite of walking on fire, I have had the honor of witnessing the passage, and sometimes even the dance on coals, of thousands of people of all ages after only a few hours of preparation.

In these moments, I cannot but ask myself, "What else can we do? What other talents and capabilities—still unknown—might we possess?"

And how can we apply them in our daily life to make it more satisfying?

How much time do we dedicate to knowing, to training, to developing our talents? Are we following our dreams? I think that trying to give an answer to these questions is not only a right but also an obligation for every one of us.

A PERFECT COMPUTER

We are all born with a very powerful perfect computer: our mind-body system. If you were given a sophisticated computer, capable of doing many functions and of improving life, wouldn't you try to use it well? Like elementary school students who find themselves in a classroom with nuclear engineers, we often use our computer without having the slightest idea of what we're doing, of the keys that we're pressing or of the programs that we're installing. In most cases, we don't even think to look for the instruction manuals. Invariably, we end up complaining that the computer is broken. Tony Buzan tells of a research study, involving thousands of people all over the world, that hoped to discover how many people knew the function of the human brain. Here is the result: 50 to 70 percent of the people interviewed knew that there was a superior and inferior part of the brain, a left and a right part, but only a few had an idea of what these areas did, and less than 1 percent had ever done something to improve their own mental and emotional potential!

Apparently, life appeared on earth about 3,500,000 years ago, but, only in the last 150 years have scientists begun to discover the true potential of our mind. And, moreover, 95 percent of the knowledge that human beings possess about the mechanisms of the brain have been discovered only in the last ten years.

We are still far from completely understanding the complex interaction of the cerebral cells. But what we do know with certainty is that the activity of the brain is formed by complex processes that cause interactions between the chemical changes of our body and that strongly influence our health, emotions and mood. It is estimated that there are about one hundred million brain cells or neurons in the human brain. As Luigi Anolli and Paolo Legrenzi explain in their book *General Psychology*, they are all present at birth, and all come from a single cell, a fertilized egg. That means that during nine months of fetal life, the formation of the brain cells proceeds at an average speed of 250,000 neurons per minute! After birth, and especially in the critical moments of development, some of the original neurons die, as do many synapses, and the connection between one neuron and another is formed and modified. It seems that after fetal development, the neurons that die are not replaced by new cells, but some of their parts, as soon as they are damaged or worn out, are replaced. A neuron can receive impulses from hundreds or thousands of connections every second. It's as if it were a kind of enormous and precise telephone switchboard, which can calculate instantaneously all the data received and then redirect it to other cells where physical, chemical, mental or emotional responses are initiated.

If we examined a portion of the brain only as small as a billiard ball and we counted the possible neural connections between the various cerebral cells, we would discover that there are many more than all the telephone networks in the whole world.

In 1973, Professor Pyotr Kuzmich Anokhin of the University of Moscow wrote an essay on the results of his sixty years of research on the human brain entitled *The Forming of Natural and Artificial Intelligence* where he wrote, "We can show that every one of the ten million neurons in the human brain has the possibility to connect 1-with-28-zeros times."

If a single neuron has that potential, we can hardly imagine what the whole brain can do.

A human being capable of using his body-mind system to its full potential doesn't exist yet. According to William James, the father of American psychology, we probably use 10 percent at the most. A question automatically comes to mind: What about the rest?

We're only human in the end.

In another study, which lasted more than thirty years and involved people in more than fifty countries, Buzan's team asked the individuals to imagine situations in which they had committed a great error and had to apologize and admit their responsibility. How would you respond in a situation like that? What words would you use to excuse yourself?

In every group, of every age, in every country, most of the people declared something like this: "I guess I'm only human." Would you have ever said that?

The conviction that, as human beings, we have many limitations and we are inclined to make mistakes is decidedly common and quite generalized.

Actually, as human as we may be, we are unique, extraordinary and miraculous creatures. I agree with Buzan, who, in his book *Let's Use Our Head,* states that the majority of our errors and failures don't depend on the fact that "we are only human;" it depends on the fact that we are only at the beginning stages of research on how we can train the incredible potential that we have as a birth right.

And, as the statistics demonstrate, many of us have never had any specific training at all.

Every human being possesses an immense potential. It is our responsibility to develop it the best we can so we can live a life full of significance and satisfaction.

The first step of this process is that of knowledge. In this case, it is the knowledge of our cognitive system and the way we form our beliefs and convictions and how they interact with our thoughts, actions and emotions.

It is necessary to understand how our mind works before we can make it work better.

CHAPTER 3

THE FRAMES OF THE MIND

The majority of computers have instruction manuals. The human mind does not.

—Phil Laut

THE HIGHLIGHTER

Imagine a small child who sees a highlighter for the first time in his life. Naturally, he picks it up, puts it in his mouth, smells it, and then starts to scribble with it on the wall. Then maybe he hears his mother coming to tell him, "It's a highlighter."

In short, what happens is very similar to data being entered into a computer. Through the five senses,[3] the nervous system of the child sends the information to the brain where it is catalogued.

Later, when the child sees a highlighter or something similar again, his computer will turn on the image containing all the information about that highlighter and he will recognize the object.

THE STOVE

Now let's imagine the same child who goes with his mother to visit his grandfather for Christmas. The only heat in the house comes from a big wood stove. He has never seen a stove in his whole life and curiously goes up to it and puts his hands on the incandescent walls.

The mother turns and screams, "No, the stove will burn you!" but it is too late. The child learns about the stove through his five senses, but, at the same time, he also has the experience of extreme pain.

Together with the data about the stove, the sensation of pain will be added to his internal computer. Later, when the mother and the child go back to visit the grandfather, do you think the child touches the stove?

---

[3] Aristotle was the first to write about the five senses. The latest studies of neuroscience were discovered by others and related to the perception of the passage of time, barometric pressure, blood pressure, body temperature, gravity, equilibrium, kinesthesia and so on. Now there are schools of thought that there are ten senses, for others twenty-one and for some even forty-four!

THE SPIDER

Now, the same child is playing in his room where he sees a big spider coming closer and closer. The child is curious, extends his hand, and the new toy climbs on his little arm. His senses, completely open and relaxed, he feels a sweet tickle on his body.

His mother decides to check up on him. She finds an enormous black spider dangerously still and only inches away from her dear son. It is then that she shouts, rushes toward her child and takes the beast from his arm.

What happens to the child? The information about the spider was tranquilly reaching his brain via his nervous system when, at the same time, comes his mother's scream. To this, her fearful hug is added.

Years later, as an adolescent, the child goes camping and an enormous black spider with furry legs enters his tent. It's easy to imagine his reaction.

Our experiences unconsciously condition our interpretations of reality and our responses to events. Every one of us brings along thousands of these reference points. Problems begin when these conditions are about things like self—trust, values, our capacity, our money, sex and interpersonal relationships.

THE MATRIX

> *The mind is like a parachute; it only works when it's open.*
>
> —*Sir James Dewar, British physicist and chemist*

When they brought me Eragon, he was about five days old and did not even know how to meow. Even if the little thing stimulated all my maternal instincts, there were certain things that I just did not know how to transmit. How could I teach him how to meow? To clean himself by licking his fur? Yet, in a few months, he began to clean himself, meow and even hunt. He had never seen it done; no one had ever taught him. It was pure instinct. Do we work in the same way? It doesn't seem so.

Abraham Maslow, one of the fathers of human psychology, believed that, contrary to animals, humans do not possess innate instincts. At most, we are born with tendencies of behavior.

Unlike Eragon, who, although brought up by humans, was able to become a cat, in cases where babies are brought up by wolves, none that have been found, except after the earliest years of life, were able to become humans. None learned how to talk, to walk on two feet, to eat anything other than roots and berries. We are not born knowing how to be human or how to live and behave with others. To learn how to become a human, we must observe, imitate, have models, experiment and classify everything.

MAKERS OF MEANINGS

According to psychology, it is within the first three years of life that we decide what it means to be a man or a woman, how we will behave as future wives, mothers, husbands, lovers, friends and workers.

Thus, we begin to define the experiences through which we will live and those which we will avoid at all cost.

William James, founder of American psychology, compared our mind to a river of consciousness.

Thoughts, emotions, memories, imagination, worries and excitement all flow together to this river of consciousness, often at the same time, sometimes rapidly and agitated, sometimes calmly and tranquilly. It is in this way that we form the frames of our mind, and through our thoughts and interpretations, we frame every event giving each its own particular significance. In this way, we, as humans, are truly "makers of meanings." In other words, we give significance, consciously or not, to every reality that we meet. We begin to generate emotion: for example, not only are we worried, but we are angry, and then we are afraid of our anger and then ashamed of our fear of our anger and so on—infinitely.

Think about the word bread. What comes to mind? The shape of the typical French baguette? The aroma of bread just taken from the oven? Breakfast? If you think of all of this, what do you feel? Hunger? Indifference? Annoyance? Nostalgia?

The word bread is an arbitrary term that represents a type of food. But how many different meanings can it have? How many symbols and mental associations can it evoke?

During the courses, I often ask the participants to write twenty words that, for them, mean house, work or vacation.

The results are surprising: independent of where they come from, of their age or of the kind of work they do, it is difficult that the words are the same.[4] Everyone associated these terms to different significances. Once I asked two people who worked in the same place to do this exercise. For the word "house," the first person's list had associations such as warmth, refuge, tranquility, well-being, relaxation and fireplace. The list of the second person included anxiety, worry,

---

[4]   For "equal" I mean exactly the same word, not variations of the same theme because that means that they have different interpretations. For example, if a person associates the word "rest" with "house" and another associates "sleep," they are not considered the same. To rest doesn't necessarily mean to sleep.

tension, work, risk, and stress. He had just taken out a mortgage that he could barely pay.

THOUGHT, EMOTION, ACTION

To any external stimulus, our mind begins taking a movie that puts us in a determined mood. Our choices and our behaviors depend on that film, from our interpretations of reality and from the significance that we give it. As you can imagine, in the case of the two workers, the word "house" produced two very different films.

In what way does the significance that we give to events influence our behavior? How does our mind-body express our interior films?

Michael Hall, founder of Neuro-Semantics, introduced the concept of "Matrix", or, better yet, matrices. Matrix is a model, an interpretive grid that allows us to work with the complexities of the human experience. By entering the matrix and examining it, we are able to pigeonhole, analyze and understand the highlights of the interior and exterior parts of our lives.

EXACTLY WHAT IS THE MATRIX?

The word matrix comes from the Latin "Mater," or mother. It is the matrix of our mind. Do you remember the film with Keanu Reeves in the role of Neo? Here's part of the explanation that Morpheus gave regarding the matrix when they met: "Matrix is the world that has been put before your eyes to hide the truth. It is a prison of the mind. An interactive stimulation of the neurons, a world of dreams where we live, the inside of a map, not the territory."

Matrix is everything around us; it's the world in which we live and that we perceive as "reality." It is the result of all the frames and the significances that we have attributed to things, people, ideas and experiences. It is the virtual universe where we have catalogued and given every event a sense and value.[5]

We were all born into a matrix of frames. The frames are built by the language that we learned, in the family to which we were born, in the culture that we assimilated, the educational system that guided what and how we studied. All these realities existed before we were born and became the cultural matrix, or womb, into which we were born. It is from the matrix we extract our reference points.

OUR FIRST ANNIVERSARY

It was our first anniversary and Nicola promised to take me out to dinner. I was really excited about the romantic evening and took my time to get ready. Returning home, he took a quick shower and changed. But, instead of leaving for dinner, he went to his study.

He turned on his computer, and, after a while, began to make phone calls.

Pretty soon, I started to feel that his work always came first—even ahead of our first anniversary. And then the fight started.

During the discussion, I found out that Nicola had turned on the computer to find the restaurant's address. Unable to find its location, he decided to call the restaurant for directions. It was an important evening, and he did not want to get lost in traffic. I felt stupid.

What is the mechanism that made it happen? The answer is the matrix: when I was little, my father would come home and often shut himself in his study to finish some jobs, to

---

[5]   *The Matrix Model: The 7 Matrices of Neuro-Semantics*, Michael Hall.

make calls or to simply relax and wind down for a few minutes. But I saw things differently. For me, it meant that I was not important enough and that he did not love me. I felt neglected. And look what happened. I immediately gave the same interpretation to Nicola's behavior.

OPPRESSED OR ABANDONED?

A few years ago, I worked with a couple who were going through a period of crisis, so much so that they were thinking of getting a separation. The arguments started mostly when one of them was not well. In those cases, Albert could not stand Lorella, whom he considered oppressive and suffocating. She, in turn, felt completely abandoned and neglected by her husband when she was not well. This provoked a deep resentment in both of them that extended into every part of their relationship. When we explored the matrices of these behaviors, we found that whenever someone was not well in Lorella's family, whether it was physical or psychological, the entire family came to the aid of the person. The person was never left alone, always had someone to talk to and even had food brought to them in their room. Every one of their needs was thought of in advance.

Albert, on the contrary, came from a family where autonomy ruled, independence and liberty being their main values. When a family member was going through a difficult moment, he was left alone. The idea was that he needed privacy, peace and quiet and tranquility in order to heal.

In the critical moments of their lives, Albert and Lorella behaved according to the frameworks that were created during their childhood. When the significance that we give events differs from that of the people around us, we usually waste time and energy trying to prove that we are right. And that's what Albert and Lorella did.

In this case, who was right? Obviously both were.

They navigated their own matrix with their own compass on board. There are no two matrices that are the same, and every time two people form a relationship, there are two different matrices, or actually two different worlds, that meet—often clashing.

THE INSTRUCTION MANUAL

> *Remember that thoughts are things that, depending on their direction, can become criminal or miracles.*
>
> *—Edgar Cayce*

How is the matrix formed? Why do we give certain significance to some events rather than to others?

As Mihaly Csikscentmihalyi tells us in his book, *Good Business,* the most recent studies of neuroscience tell us that the brain can process about thirty million pieces of information a second, but, at the conscious level, we can only process a small part.

SEVEN PLUS OR MINUS TWO

Already in 1956, the psychologist George Miller had analyzed the amount of information that man must decipher consciously and decided that it was about seven units at a time. In 2001, Cowen, another psychologist, corrected this, saying that the amount of data that we can process and remember is about four chunks at a time.

Think about everything that you have ever done, said, seen, eaten, touched, smelled, listened to from the time you woke up this morning. Do you remember every single thing down to the details? Is it impossible?

The human brain computes about a million operations a second and our mind cannot process everything consciously. Unable to process all the information, the most important is chosen. It's as if we wanted to take an immense panoramic photo and we had to decide what to focus on, which particulars to zoom in on—but we do it unconsciously.

We can compare the conscious part of our mind to the tip of an iceberg and the unconscious part to the vast part that is underwater.

Most information is transferred directly to the unconscious, the part under water, which has infinite possibilities. This transfer is pretty much an automatic process, made up of generalizations, distortions and cancellations, all of which we will look at later.

THE ERRORS OF THOUGHT AND THE 3PS

In 1975, psychologists Albert Ellis and Robert Harper (and Aaron Beck in 1983), while completing a study on Rational Emotional Behavior Therapy (RET), called these functions of the mind "cognitive distortions or errors of thought"—or the ways we reason unproductively.

In that vein, in his book *To Learn,* Seligman offers his readers a recipe to ensure unhappiness. This recipe is called the 3Ps. You don't have to do anything but start to *personalize* the significance to events, especially negative ones, and make them *pervasive* and *permanent.*

Nancy, a dear friend of mine, is a true champion of *personalization.* As long as someone does not answer her mail within 24 hours, she quickly believes that the person is angry with her. When her son decided to leave university to dedicate himself to organic farming, she thought that he did it to go against her. If someone asks her advice but then does not use it, she considers it a personal insult. Every time I talk to her, something bad has happened (it's always her).

My reaction to Nicola the day of our first anniversary was, however, a classic example of *pervasiveness*. The data initially entered in our computer is very specific, in my case my relationship with my father. Very soon, however, the idea and the context are forgotten. The conviction is formed and then replicated and sent to other contexts, in my case to my relationship with Nicola. When the puppy you just adopted pees on your favorite carpet, do you quickly think that you should take him back to the pound because he will never learn? You go back to the gym after quite a few months of inactivity and you pull a muscle in your back. Do you decide that sports are not for you because you just keep getting hurt anyway? These are examples of *permanence*. They will surely not make your life better.

In observing your behavior, do you note recurring themes? When faced with certain external stimuli—when your partner scolds you or a colleague continuously asks for help—do you find yourself reacting the same way? It's very probable that that way of thinking has become a habit for you and has become automatic and you don't even realize it.

Do you tend to jump to conclusions or judge too quickly? Do you see everything in terms of black and white, right or wrong? Do you let a negative experience ruin your whole day? Do you make terrible prophecies and imagine the worst scenario? Welcome to the group of champions of cognitive distortions!

ARE YOU READY TO ENTER THE MATRIX?

> *If reality is what you can feel, smell, touch and see, then what you call real is only electrical signals interpreted by your brain.*
>
> —*Morpheus,* The Matrix

Until it is stimulated, the matrix is dormant. The matrix is activated when we smell a perfume, receive a telephone call or find ourselves blocked in traffic. In the moment, in which it is triggered, it governs our mood and, consequently, our actions.

What is the matrix that frames your mind like? Is it helpful to you in achieving well-being and reaching your goals? Does it help you have healthy satisfying relationships? Does it let you wake each morning filled with excitement for the day ahead, for your job, for your family, for yourself, for your contribution to the world?

At this point, it is easy to understand the importance of exploring our virtual world so we can do a quality control and verify exactly which frames are significant and functional and which are not.

I'M JUST LIKE THAT; IT'S MY NATURE

Maybe some of you are thinking, "I'm just like that. It's my nature."

But where does our character come from? How is it formed? The answer always takes us to the same place: matrix! Our character is the combination of the frames, the significances that we gradually give events, the decisions that we have unconsciously made and the cognitive distortions we have used. Then, through repetition, we have trained ourselves, often for years, to behave in the same way. The frames have become stronger and more solidified, and we have become true champions of that certain behavior.

Probably, there have even been some with positive results.

If, however, we are not living exactly the way we want, the good news is that we can train ourselves to change parts that we want to, in the same way that we trained to create our character in the first place. The matrix, in fact, is not a static system but a true, real and continually growing world. If we want the matrix to stop guiding our actions from the depths of our unconscious, the first thing we must do is enter it and understand it. But normally, the matrix is hidden so we must learn to see it.

Only by knowledge can we realize its reality. Only when we bring it to a conscious level can we attest to and verify its contents. Then, finally, the toxic frames can be discussed and modified.

QUALITY CONTROL

Probably you're thinking, "Does this not happen automatically?" No, it does not. The human brain does not perform any kind of quality control—at least not automatically.

The brain behaves more stupidly than the stomach. If we try to feed it with garbage, our stomach is intelligent enough to realize immediately and will push us to quickly expel the poison.

The brain does not do that. It nurtures itself with whatever is given. This is when we must acknowledge and voluntarily and consciously activate quality control. In the following pages, we will enter the matrix and every one of us will have the possibility to explore their own.[6] During this activity, we will encounter beliefs, which we have framed, often distorting reality.

If you do the exercises and answer the questions, you will realize how you have mapped your experiences, what frames

---

[6] Matrix is basically a model, and, as Dr. Hall sustains, no model is real or absolute. No model is "the truth". Models are merely maps that we use to explore reality. Matrix is, however, a useful model that allows us to explore and reconstruct the sophisticated world that we have built within ourselves.

and significance you have given to yourself. You will be able to see that you have associated certain responses to certain stimuli and that certain ways of thinking have taken over your mind so much that it actually identifies you. And, even more so, you will understand which of these frames are useful and help you live well and which do not.

To be able to explore this content more efficiently, the matrix is subdivided into five areas.[7] It is in these virtual places where beliefs, values and convictions are born and live. During this journey to the inside of our matrix, our principal job will be to identify the frames that urgently need change and to discover the viruses of the mind. As long as all these meanings remain in our unconscious, they will, in fact, guide us in the wrong directions and inhibit us from developing to our full potential. As we will see better in chapter six, which is dedicated to the compass of change, awareness is the door to transformation. The first step toward a new life is to identify the significant dysfunctional frames that, like old records, have played in our minds over and over for years. Matrix is a dynamic system and can be entered from every direction and traveled through freely, although here, we will use a method that will imitate its natural development to explore it.

At the end of the paragraphs dedicated to every single matrix, you will find a series of questions to help you explore your matrix. In addition, for every matrix, the general questions are: Do you know the frame in which you operate? Is this the best frame to use? Would you like to establish a different frame? Which one might it be?

---

[7] What we will see is only a part of Dr. Hall's work and has been simplified and modified to make it easier and more immediately useful. The complete Matrix Model is actually formed of content matrices (here to follow) and process matrices (intention and significance) but, in the book, they are treated separately.

The best way to make this journey is to take a few minutes when you will not be disturbed. Take your diary, a pen; read the questions one at a time and let your answers come to mind. Don't judge the thoughts that come to you; simply write them down on a piece of paper. At the end, after you have completed the whole series of questions, reread everything that you have written. In doing this, you will be able to notice that certain significances, or frames, influence many areas of your life. And you will discover that when we modify a frame in a determined way, the change has an effect, systemically, on other areas as well.

Are you ready to enter the matrix?

THE MATRIX OF SELF

> *As you walk, going down every road, you will never reach the end of your soul, so deep is its essence.*

> *—Eraclito*

The first person with whom we come into contact is ourselves. It is only with ourselves that we are certain to be with twenty four out of twenty four hours a day—from the time we are born until the moment we die. We should not be surprised then, if, upon entering the matrix, the first area that we enter is that of Self. The convictions regarding ourselves influence every area of our life and our relationships. This is the first matrix that is activated and the one we use to relate to the world from the time we are babies and begin to ask ourselves: Who am I? Am I ok? Am I a lovable person, likable? Very soon, those around us—our parents, our teachers—begin to put labels on our identity—you are good, you are bad, you're intelligent, you're stupid. It is here that all the significances and the definitions that we have given to ourselves are registered and define who we are.

It is in this matrix that every one of our actions has a beginning, at least in part.

And, in this area of the matrix, we find the trust and love for ourselves, the values with which we identify ourselves, and the way in which we talk to ourselves.

It is here that self-esteem originates, on which, unfortunately, there is still a lot of confusion.

AAA...WANTED SELF-ESTEEM

> *No psychological health is possible unless the essential core of every person is fundamentally accepted, loved and respected.*
>
> —*Abraham Maslow*

When I was a model, every time I had a successful job I felt something in me grow, which I thought was self-esteem. I think it's a common mechanism. I see it in action in many people: professionals, sportsmen, or simply proud parents on the outcome of their children. Every time we get results, our self-esteem increases.

For a long time, even after having started my current job, such as when the participants in my courses achieved the results they wanted quickly, I gave myself a pat on the back and told myself, "You did it! I'm really proud of you!"

Every victory of my clients was a personal victory for me. And that helped me keep a high self-esteem.

But life is always ready with new lessons. One day, fifty-year-old Marilena, ill with cancer, arrived in class wanting to learn how to better manage her emotions regarding her illness. At that time, I was a teacher of her techniques and some participants in my courses were actually able to debilitate cancer. Maybe because of this, my goal was to help Marilena become well. A few months later, to my complete surprise, she died. For me, I was a complete failure. It did not matter that Marilena had died peacefully, having made peace with her family after having been at odds with them for her whole life.

In my eyes, I had not reached my goal. I was not good enough to aid a person who had asked for my help. So I was worth nothing. All of a sudden, my self-esteem hit rock bottom. After a period of complete dejection, when I questioned my whole profession, I realized that there must have been a mistake in the way I was looking at things. How could an external event have so greatly influenced what I thought of myself?

Thanks to that episode, I began to really understand what self-esteem is, above and beyond the many new age theory, which are often too superficial. Many, as did I, confuse self-esteem with self-efficiency or faith in oneself. Others believe that the sense of well being induced by that self-esteem is gained by the approval and esteem of others.

Well, self-esteem is neither of these.

Maybe, the confusion comes from the term esteem. To esteem (appraise) implies making a valuation. But what is the value of a human being? And which expert will do that appraisal? What tool should we use for this measurement? Depending on the culture, it could be money, the brain, beauty, character or designer clothes, and so on. Have you asked yourself which scale of measurement you're using for yourself?

Regardless of which method you choose, the problem is that it is influenced. It's only worthwhile if you respect certain conditions that, however, can change or be taken away at any moment. These conditions, as Buddhism teaches, are not permanent.

So, from one day to the next, you will be able to see your values crumble in the worldwide stock market of human beings.

So what should we do? Why not start by giving an unconditional value to each human being, as we will see on the 3A path?

It is an intrinsic value of the self-matrix, a birthright that no one can take away. What is your worth?

It means to celebrate and honor who we are as human beings, independent of what we do (career, age, physical aspect, money), as we will see in the matrix of personal power, and independent of anyone else's approval, as we will see in the matrix of others.

We don't have to wait for permission to do this. We don't have to wait until we reach a certain objective. We can simply decide to feel that way—now—in this precise moment. Keep telling yourself that you can: "I have nothing to prove and everything to experiment. I am as worthy as any other human being, simply because I exist."

As we will see, it is an awareness that no one else can give you. It has to come from you. That's why it's called self-esteem and not 'esteem of others.'

To develop self-esteem, you must make a sharp distinction between people and behavior. When we learn to separate being from doing, we can be dissatisfied or not proud of our achievements, and yet, we can continue to love ourselves and value ourselves as human beings. If we make a mistake, it does not mean that we are a mistake. If we find ourselves behaving selfishly, and selfishness is something that we don't like, it is the selfishness that we disapprove us—not ourselves. If we think we are incompetent, it is the incompetence that we must fight—not ourselves.

This is, obviously, true for others as well. If someone does something bad, it is the bad that we must hate—not the person. We are much more than our behaviors, our achievements, our actions, and, if we identify with them, we will end up suffering.

To make mistakes is normal and is part of the process of learning. We cannot expect to never make a mistake. Perfectionism blocks action and prohibits personal development with its straight jacket. It is only when we allow ourselves to be imperfect, to make mistakes, to try and retry that we can evolve and improve. But we are free to do it only when we do not doubt our worth as a human being. If, on the other hand, we think our worth is connected to our behavior, our job, our achievements, our income or our physical aspect, we will end up being very disappointed.

But what information does our personal matrix contain?

I'M NOT WORTH ANYTHING

Imagine a child being questioned at school. The response from the teacher is 'insufficient'—or a red 'D' may be written in the student's notebook.

Do you think it's easy for that child to understand that the grade of 'insufficient' is not connected to his own identity or to his behavior—but simply to his studying for the presentation of that lesson?

Or is it more probable, especially if this scenario repeats itself, that the child registers in his personal matrix that he, himself, is insufficient and is worth only a 'D'?

And every time he finds himself in a similar situation, even as an adult, when he is asked to make a presentation, or when he wants to .ask his boss for a raise, his mind goes back to the thought that he is 'insufficient, not worthy enough.' It makes his mouth go dry, gives him shortness of breath, and makes him relive the tension and the fear of that grade.

This is only an example. How often do we hear or say of ourselves: you're bad, you're selfish, you're insensitive? These are true labels that remain attached to your identity. Wouldn't it be better to say that it is the behavior that is selfish, bad or insensitive and not the person himself?

THE 3AS

This specific path toward self-esteem was developed by Neuro-Semantics, and, for many years, we have used it in our seminars with great success. It is composed of three phases known as the 3As: acceptance, appreciation and admiration.

To begin, we must learn to accept our errors. We have seen that this is a very important step, not only for external situations, but especially, for the parts of ourselves that we don't love. Imagine giving a speech in front of hundreds of managers, mostly men. You're on the stage with all the spotlights pointed at you. In the highlight of your speech, the words you use—in Spanish—to mean 'and now open your eyes', mean, 'open your pants'. You wanted to gradually bring the audience out of a meditative state; instead, you caused overall laughing.

This happened to me, and it was not pleasant. Years ago, I could have fallen through the stage floor, and I would never have come out if I had had my way. Fortunately for me, I had been working for a while with the exercise of the 3As. So I said to myself that it was not pleasant, but it's not the end of the world. Just as we accept a rainy day or having to clean the bathroom, we can also accept having made a fool of ourselves. I am not a fool. I am much more.

This behavior helps us distance ourselves and avoid the feeling of having to defend ourselves. It allows us to accept our errors and quickly bounce back.

The second step is to begin to notice and appreciate every effort that we make, every trial, independent of the result, in the same way that we appreciate good food or the company of friends. This will help us to enjoy our small advances and will urge us to improve. Unfortunately, we are often so concentrated on our faults that we forget to appreciate our good points. We will talk more about this in the chapter dedicated to the tools of transformation.

The third step toward self-esteem is admiration. Imagine holding a newborn. Look at his little hands, his eyes; touch his soft delicate skin and hear his cooing from his smiling face. What do you feel? Joy? Love? Wonder? Admiration?

And yet, that baby does nothing but sleeps and eats. It does not bring money home, does not take care of the family; it's not better than others nor does it reach achievements in any particular area. The baby does nothing to be loved and approved. But we watch him, filled with love, because our admiration is not because of his achievements. It is for what he is: a small human being. Why do we stop feeling that same wonder and celebration of who we are as grown adults? Why, as adults, do we use achievements as measurements of self-worth and love?

As a child, I often spent time watching, in awe, the perfection of nature. I could not wrap my mind around how every flower had its own precise color and shape, its own typical perfume, its own exact time to bloom. Every time I watched the animals on the African savanna, I was breathless. And what about the giraffes with their long necks, perfect for reaching the highest tops of trees? And the incredible colors at sunset? What is behind all this perfection!?

I strongly feel this sense of wonder and admiration every time I am in nature, but for years I did not realize that we, too, are part of the same. That same vital energy flows, even in us. The beauty of a sunset is the same as our beauty. The perfection that governs the various aspects of nature makes us unique examples as well.

The same intelligence is within us, each and every one, so much so that we are capable of creating life. What more proof do we need to recognize our essence and honor it? When we observe the perfection of a newborn human, we feel we want to celebrate life, the same that is within ourselves. Maybe that's why we love little children so much—because it's easier to recognize beauty in them. Can you recognize the beauty of human nature by looking at your own? Are you capable of seeing how precious, mysterious, miraculous and sacred you are?

GLORIOUSLY FALLIBLE

Unconditionally feeling our worth as human beings frees us from the need to prove anything to anyone. If we are unconditionally worthy, we are free to be gloriously fallible. Being imperfect, we possess the right to err and to make mistakes without it taking anything away from our self-worth. How would things change if our admiration for who we are was at the base of the foundation of the matrix of our 'self?' How would we react to errors and failures if love and esteem were never doubted? How would our choices change if we had nothing to prove to ourselves or to the world—and everything to experiment?

EXPLORATION OF THE MATRIX OF SELF

Answer the following questions in your diary and discover the identity that you have given yourself.

- What do you think of yourself?
- Who are you? How are you? What aren't you?

- How would you define yourself? What is your nature?
- Does the way you define yourself help you?
- Does it make your life better? Does it give you power?

YOUR WORTH

Do you like yourself? What do you accept (or not accept) about yourself? What do you appreciate? Is the worth that you give yourself conditioned? If yes, by what? (I love myself if/ when...) What happens if these conditions are missing? Is that useful? Do you need it? If yes, for what?

THE 3AS OF SELF-ESTEEM

For this exercise, take at least ten minutes with no one around to disturb you and read the following phrases, allowing yourself to follow your own voice.

Log in to a state of *acceptance*. Remember a moment in which you have accepted something, even something small and simple. What small things could you accept without really liking them or wanting to, but which you could welcome? A rainy day, traffic, paying bills, cleaning the bathroom, etc. Go to that state of simple acceptance for what it is. Remember a moment when you felt appreciation. When you really welcomed something with enthusiasm in your life. A good meal, the company of friends, a vacation? What moves you while you are appreciating it? Love for the people who are closest to you, watching a work of art? Do you feel the appreciation?

Now, go to a moment in which you felt *admiration*. Does something so marvelous exist, so incredible, that it leaves you in absolute admiration? The hands of a newborn, the perfume of fresh musk in the woods after the rain. Do you feel a sensation of admiration and respect?

Now, go back to the feeling of *acceptance*. How do you look when you are accepted? What feelings do you have?

Do what you must to amplify this state of acceptance until you feel it very powerfully. When it is the strongest, throw your anchor, close your fists or touch a hand and do what you must to anchor your body to this sensation of acceptance.

While you have your anchor, apply this sensation of acceptance to the things in your life that you know are good to accept, but that, up to now, you have found difficult to accept, like your dark side or your weak points. Up to now, you have perceived these as errors, actions, behaviors, moods, words of which you are not proud. They might not be perfect or what you wanted, but, in any case, continue to anchor them to this sensation of acceptance. Accept everything as you would a rainy day. Accept the experiences that you have had, the cards that life has dealt you. Accept everything; accept your absolute sense of self and of life.

Now go to the feeling of appreciation. How do you look when you feel appreciated? What do you feel? Do what is necessary to amplify how you feel when you are appreciated until you feel it very powerfully. When it is the strongest it can get, close your fist or do what you must to anchor this sensation of appreciation to yourself.

While you still have your anchor, apply this sensation of appreciation to your sense of self as a person who acts and conquers. Appreciate your sense of self in its totality, in what it does, in the gifts that life has given you, in your talents, in your strong points, in the goals you have achieved, in all the beautiful things in your life; look at them, feel them and appreciate them one by one.

Now go to the feeling of admiration. How do you look when admired? How do you feel? Do what you must to amplify how you feel when admired until you feel it quite powerfully. When it is at its strongest, close your fist or do whatever you have to do to anchor this feeling of admiration in your whole body.

While you have your anchor, apply this feeling of admiration and respect of yourself, the magnificent and precious human being of unconditional value that you are. Bring respect, esteem and admiration to the mystery of who you really are, to your potential, to your essence as a human being, to your soul, to your heart.

Continuing to completely and fully perceive this respect of yourself, let it grow and expand. While you hold the anchor, think of what other things you could appreciate and what other things you could accept gracefully and easily. You can let the anchor go now.

Is there one context, situation or event in which you are not loved, find disapproval of yourself or have doubted your potential and your worth?

In which area do you wish you had more resources?

While you are thinking, I want you to re-launch your anchor and feel the esteem you have for yourself. I want you to know that you are valuable and worth a lot and that you feel this appreciation so much that you can focus on redirection and accepting certain things.

Now observe the way feeling this esteem and self- admiration of your personal mysteries and of your potential transforms your old feelings.

- Do you like it? Can this make a difference?
- Are you ready to respect yourself—
  no matter what happens?
- Use your imagination to take all of this to the future.
- Imagine moving through your life, in the weeks and months to come, with this frame of mind. Do you like it?
- Observe things that could change for you.

- Are even the highest parts of your mind in agreement?
- Would you like to continue this way?

THE MATRIX OF PERSONAL POWER

> *If you plan to be less than you are capable of, I warn that you will be deeply unhappy for the rest of your life.*
>
> —*Abraham Maslow*

The matrix of personal power is strongly attached to the matrix of self. From the time we were born, we began to move, immediately trying to discover what we were able to do and to test our capacity. In this way, we began to receive feedback on our efficiencies and to form convictions about our ability.

In this matrix, we find our resources and our potential, our possibility of choice and the capacity to solve problems, along with the significance that we gave to our limits and weaknesses. If self-esteem has to do with the matrix o f self along with its self-sufficiency and its faith in your own efficiency, it also has to do with the matrix of personal power.

DO YOU HAVE FAITH IN YOUR CAPACITIES?

While self-esteem is tied to being, self-efficacy is tied to doing. It is conditioned by the results that we get. It develops gradually and grows slowly as we become competent in what we do. We can have faith in our ability to earn money, to make friends, to express our sexuality or a million other things. Remember, everything that has to do with faith in ourselves is not self-esteem.

We can have a strong sense of auto-efficacy in one area but not in another. For example, I have faith in my capacity to give classes and to speak in public, but I have none in my ability to cook or paint. I am very good at speaking English, French and Spanish but not Russian, German or Arabic.

Developing faith in our capacities helps us realize that we can make it in life. This is important because it allows us not only to accept our destiny, whatever it may be, but to also make it the best we can.

Martin Seligman did an experiment, which will help us understand how auto-efficacy is born. His team put some dogs, one at a time, in a box that had no escape. They put other dogs into an open box from which they could easily get out. Then they gave each group of animals a light electric shock through the floor of the box. The dogs in the open box very quickly learned how to get out and be safe, while the dogs in the closed box stopped trying to get out after a while and stretched out passively on the floor accepting their destiny. They had learned resignation.

Then all the dogs were put in a box with two compartments. In one area, there was an electric shock and, in the other, there was not. The dogs, which had been in the open box earlier, discovered quickly how to get to the safe zone. Most of the dogs which had been in the closed box earlier stayed in the area with the electric shocks without even trying to escape. They were used to the idea and had no hope.

Unfortunately, this phenomenon does not relate only to animals. When the feeling of auto-efficacy is depleted, unimaginable damage is done. As Dan Baker sustains, in his book *I Want to be Happy*, when people feel incapable of managing their own environment, their instinct for survival is threatened. This brings on high psychological stress that creates anxiety and depression, reactions that then increase the conviction that the person is not capable of making it.

Did you grow up in a social context, in the family and in school, which supported and encouraged your talents?

Did you feel safe to explore and use your power? Or did you live in a chaotic environment where the people had unpredictable reactions, where you were criticized, hollered at or unjustly punished?

Do you happen to behave in one of the following ways, especially when under stress? Do you:

- Think you're never going to be able to change things?
- Feel passive, have no energy, see yourself as a victim of events over which you have no power?
- Use complaining as your main topic of conversation?
- Believe that others were luckier?
- Think that someone should help you or resolve things for you?
- Blame others for your situation (your partner, the government, your boss, your colleagues, the city where you live?)
- often use the words "if only...(I were young, had more money, had more help, etc.), I don't have to, I can't, it won't matter anyway"?
- Need to have everything under control?
- Attack others?
- Want to show that you are the strongest no matter what?

CAUTION! These are real and true traps that inhibit your personal power and block your ability to change. When you realize that you are behaving this way, STOP!

WHATEVER I DO NEVER GOES RIGHT

There are reactions that rise from the dysfunctional contents of the matrix. If, as a child, the significance we attributed to criticism and failure was, "So what! Anything I do is never good; I'm not capable, so it's better if I just resign myself to the fact since I have no other choice," most probably, having difficulty striving for great objectives because we will think that we're not capable of reaching them. Sometimes the sensation of survival is to resign ourselves to what we have rather than living fully. We work hard to say, "no" to people and situations, and we let others or events control our lives.

Feeling helpless and thinking that there is no other choice, we often do the same job that we don't like for our whole lives or live in a city that we hate and so on.

LIFE IS A STRUGGLE

It's also possible that childhood experiences are reacted to in the opposite way, ending up at the opposite extreme. We decide that life is a struggle and it's better to attack before being attacked. In order to not feel incapable, we believe ourselves invincible. Our whole life is spent searching for power, such as social ranking, money, fame or beauty. Through these, we have the illusion of power to avoid suffering. We believe that we must direct the universe. We feel the need to have everything under control. Sometimes, we become authoritarian, manipulating or arrogant, but we do it because we believe that, in certain cases, it is the only solution. In the most extreme cases, we are convinced that life is for winners, and if someone wins, someone else must lose. We have no doubt that our self-esteem and our sense of self-sufficiency is high. In the end, we get what we want—or almost. We live this way as long as our lives don't start cracking and we fall off the pedestal. If the faith we have in our capacity is altered, we will think that each of us is a Superman being capable of doing anything, even when we are not actually capable. It might seem as though you feel fine, but your faith is deceiving you. You are tricking yourself.

Have you seen yourself in either of these descriptions? Do you know people like this? The problem is never the people.

Neither is it the events experienced, no matter how painful they were. The problem is the frames, the significances that we gave to such events. This is why twins who live the same experiences can develop completely different characters.

To cure the personal power matrix means to substitute the dysfunctional significances. It also means to assume complete responsibility for your life and to stop wasting time and energy blaming others or making them victims. In the end, we are responsible for the significances that we decide to give to our experiences and in what we choose to believe.

Certainly, such an undertaking is not for those who are passive, weak of heart, for those who are lazy or those who choose the paths of least resistance. When we heal this matrix, we become assertive and proactive, focused on solutions rather than on problems, on resources rather than on obstacles. We are determined, but flexible, and we have faith in ourselves and in our capacity to succeed. At the same time, we are honest in recognizing our errors and our improvements, and we are humble enough to learn from others. We are able to ask for help and are ready to offer it. We choose win-win situations. We decide when to say "yes" to people, experiences or ideas, and, at the same time, we are also able to create boundaries and to protect ourselves by saying, "no." We also know that if we give up the right to say "no," we can never give a completely sincere "yes."

In other words, when this matrix is balanced, we are capable of using our four powers as described in the first chapter: the power of thinking, feeling, speaking and acting.

THE EXPLORATION OF THE MATRIX OF PERSONAL POWER

- How self-responsible are you? Examine yourself. Read the following phrases and find a variety of endings.

- Keep doing this until you have come up with a dozen or so and write them in your diary as you go.
- If I assume full responsibility for all I think...
- If I assume full responsibility for all the emotions that I feel...
- If I assume full responsibility for all I say...
- If I assume full responsibility for all I do...
- What would you start thinking, feeling saying, doing? What would you stop thinking, saying, doing? (ie: stop saying yes when you feel it is a no, start asking for support, stop putting yourself down, start expressing your needs, etc)

Don't worry about whether the answers that you give are positive or negative; that's not the point. The purpose of this process is to become more knowledgeable of self-efficiency and responsibility. It will help you increase your possibility to choose and expand your personal power.

THE MATRIX OF OTHERS

> *Everything that irritates us in someone else's behavior helps us to better understand ourselves.*
>
> —*Carl Jung*

During the first months of life, a baby's mind works according to the idea that, beyond his sight, nothing exists. If mommy or daddy leaves the baby's sight, they don't exist for him anymore. That is why babies sometimes cry desperately. That is why, if you hide, you can see the newborn's face sadden and then rejoice when you reappear a second later. Then, between six and nine months, the baby begins to understand that people exist even if he can't see them. The matrix of others is born. Through thoughts and emotions, we begin to bring people with us. As time goes by, the number of people that we bring with us increases—our family members, our acquired family, wives, husbands, acquaintances, colleagues, even ex-partners, ex-colleagues and former friends.

When we are born, we depend completely on others to survive. We need to be fed, given drinks, cleaned and dressed. Alone, we are not even capable of turning ourselves over on our side. In addition to needing others as infants, as we grow, it is through the way others treat us that we get an idea of our own identity. We begin to define who we are through the way others see us. We are social beings, so it's no wonder that bonds, approval, love and emotional nourishment are so important for us.

I LOVE YOU IF...

Anna is sad, listless and not doing well in school. She is the daughter of a friend of mine, and, unlike her mother, has an outgoing personality. She loves activity, and rather than playing with dolls, she prefers soccer. She hates the classical dance and piano lessons that her mother proposes but loves to run, fight, climb trees and get dirty playing. Her parents worry, "It is not normal for a girl to behave like this. She's such a tomboy. She will never find a man."

Anna learned as a young child that love and approval are earned by behaving correctly. She quickly learned what she needed to do to get a smile and hugs or blame and criticism. When her behavior does not please her parents, Anna feels deeply wrong so she ends up complying with the standards of their requests. The unconscious dilemma for her is, "Do I betray the people I love or do I betray myself?" Regularly, she chooses to betray herself so she can have the love and approval of her parents. This is why she is sad and listless.

It is easy to imagine how this behavior will repeat itself in her adult relationships. This is known as conditional love, and we find examples of it everywhere. The key phrase to look for is, "I love you if…" even if it's not exactly said explicitly.

I love you if you behave like I want you to, if you take care of me, if you don't embarrass me, if you stop hanging out with people I don't like, if you get a full-time job, etc., and because we all want to be loved, the threat begins to work. Starving for love, we do everything including negating ourselves and giving up on our dreams just to be accepted, appreciated and loved.

But what are the results? Does this behavior make us happier? Does it make our relationships more harmonious?

REPETITION COMPULSION

It refers to doing the same things from generation to generation without even realizing it. It is a kind of psychological heredity. The way we were treated as a child is pretty much the way we will treat ourselves and others.

By observing our parents', family members' and other significant adults' behavior during our infancy, we deduced the rules for having relationships with others, how to manage our emotions and conflicts, how to communicate, negotiate, compete, collaborate and pardon. We learned when and how to love and to hug, whether or not to trust others, if it was appropriate to open up ourselves and demonstrate our vulnerabilities.

In addition, parents, as well as teachers, are our first authority figures. How do you react to authority? Are you intimidated? Do you feel hostile? Do you tend to conform or rebel?

HALF-A-DOLLAR BILL?

Mommy and daddy are also the fundamental prototypes of the man-woman relations. If, as children, we heard hollering and doors slamming, we probably associate this with our concept of a couple. What was your parents' relationship like? Were there affectionate gestures? Dialogue? Tenderness? Intimacy? In creating our own relationships as adults, we often react by behaving just the opposite—even the extreme opposite. But the relationship between our parents will always be our starting line and main reference point, even if unconsciously.

What did you learn as a child about relationships with others? About women? About men? About marriage? What do you want from a sentimental relationship? What are the qualities that you seek?

In an ideal situation, it is from our parents that we learned to go from our childhood relationships of dependence to independence. The passage is not only physical but also psychological. We are entering a stage where we are able to operate autonomously, know our own strengths and weaknesses, fight for our own dreams and love our own company.

If we don't develop this capability, we won't be able to have interdependent relationships with others or, in other words, mature relationships where each person can stand alone—whether they are friends, colleagues or partners. Khalil Gibran, poet and Sufi sage, sustained that, in a couple, the partners are like columns of the same doorway. In an adult relationship, we are not halves of the same dollar bill because, without the other half, we would be worth nothing. We are two perfectly whole bills, spendable separately, and when we are together, we are worth even more. We can experience passion, excitement, enthusiasm about the idea of seeing the other, but we don't feel threatened or impaired in their absence. Skipping this phase of independence makes us incapable of such relationships. We would go from the infantile independence to co-dependence. We would continually need others whether it was a friend, a lover, a child or colleague. In the attempt to fill the emptiness that no one else can, we would nag to get attention, company, time and approval. Or, to exorcize the fear of being abandoned, we would try, at all costs, to help, aid and save others. But, obviously, we would want to fix them in our own way and would be extremely offended if our ideas are not followed.

The opposite of all of this is Agape, the love of the benevolence and good will that works toward the happiness of all people. It is a mature love, disinterested, that loves for the pure joy of loving, of taking care of and enriching the well-being of others.

How would you define your relationships? What do you expect from the people with whom you have relationships?

THE BEST THEY COULD

This does not mean to be an attack on your family, your parents or teachers.

Some of them may have had abusive behaviors but, for the most part, they are normal human beings with their own imperfections. In the area of teaching or in bringing up children, they simply made the same number of errors as they did in other areas.

But they did the best they could, with the tools and knowledge that they had at their disposal. If this is difficult to believe, think about their childhood when they were still little and in school. You will realize that they could not have done more. They received their limited programming, and it unconsciously guided their behavior. If we don't try to change, they will guide ours too.

If we want to live a peaceful life and have stable relationships, it is important to be at peace with the matrices of others, with their childhood and their family. Know that facts
and people can influence your choices and your emotions,
but no one can control them. If you still don't believe it, there
is an area for transformation in the chapter about tools where
you will find exercises dedicated to forgiveness that you can
use toward this end.

EXPLORING THE MATRICES OF OTHERS

- What are other people like?
- What do you think about them? In general, do you think
  that they are honest, well-intentioned and friendly? Or
  are they opportunistic and potentially dangerous?
- Is it easy for you to open up to others? Do you trust
  people? Or do you think it's better to stay on your
  guard and be cautious?
- Do you start relationships easily? Or do you hold back?
- How would you define your interpersonal relationships?
- Are you happy with the way you behave in your
  relationships?
- How about your sentimental life?
- What would you like to change? What would you
  like to keep?

Complete these phrases:

- Women are…
- Men are…
- Marriage is….
- Living together is…
- My partner and I are…
- I need others when…

THE MATRIX OF TIME

It's never too late to have a happy childhood.

—Richard Bandler

Do you know anyone who always lives in the past? Or maybe someone who always lives in the future and never takes a moment to stop and smell a flower? Or someone who lives only in the present moment?

This matrix defines the way in which we relate to time and the significance that we give it. Do you have enough time or are you always under pressure? Is time a tyrant or is it your friend? Do you believe that it is an unlimited resource? Are you able to slow down or accelerate depending on the moment? Do you own time or is it time that owns you?

It is we who create time by considering things that have happened (the past), things that are happening (the present) and things that will happen (the future).

Sometimes, our distress has nothing to do with the present but is because of something that happened "in the past." The distress is "how we continue" since we keep the thoughts and feelings of the past in our mind. For example, war veterans have a hard time leading normal lives post-war as their bodies come home but their minds do not.

Where do you mainly live? Where are your thoughts? In the past, the present or the future? The time where you mostly find yourself will determine your emotions.

Whoever lives in the past, is more likely to be taken by nostalgia, depression, regrets and remorse; those who live in the present have a better chance of being impulsive and impatient but also committed and connected; those who continually project themselves to the future tend to feel tension, anxiety, and worry but also hope and desire, especially if their hopes and desires are positive. Where is it best to focus?

In the next chapters, you will find various techniques that will help you learn from the past, enjoy the present and plan for the future.

Even the significance that we give to time strongly influences our lives in every way, including our capacities.

GO SLOWLY

My father inherited the tendency to extend time the same way African countries often do. Every move he made seemed to follow a slow interior rhythm, and his attention was constantly focused on what he was doing, as if there were no tomorrow. One of his favorite expressions was "pole pole," which in Swahili meant, "slow slow." In other words, he did not like to hurry.

When I was three years old, I got my first bicycle. It was a child's model with the training wheels and the first time I got on it, my father said, "Go slowly!" It was surely good advice considering my physical capabilities. Years later, when I could learn to balance myself without the training wheels, the words my father had said resounded in my ears. "Go slowly." His advice made sense.

At sixteen, I got a motorbike. I had wanted it at fourteen but, for two years, I had to work at convincing my parents that I would go slowly. Obviously, from the very first day that I got it, my father did not hesitate to tell me to "go slowly." At eighteen, I got my license. It goes unsaid that, every time I went out with the car, I heard the whispered, "Go slowly."

For years I believed that these warnings were correct. But then I began to notice that every time even when I left by train, my father would say goodbye with his catchphrase "go slowly."

I remember one day when we were in Zambia. I was sixteen at the time and was going to go for a vacation at the beach of Dar es Salaam in Tanzania. My father took me to the airport of Lusaka and when I was about to leave, he hugged me, gave me the precious keys of the house, and, watching me climb the airplane's steps, told me to "go slowly." "In the plane?" I thought.

It goes without saying that this warning—this "go slowly"—continued to buzz around me for many years and influenced my relationship with time and the speed of action.

My mother loved the mountains in the winter, and, every year, I would go with her on a skiing vacation. During the vacation, I had lots of fun, made lots of new friends and, best of all, took skiing lessons almost every day. I followed my new friends down the slopes—but—while they were having fun launching themselves down the hills, I had trouble as soon as I started to pick up speed. I heard a thundering voice inside me saying, "Go slowly." My heart would beat quickly, my entire body became stiff and, in one second, the joy of skiing left me to be replaced by a feeling of tension and insecurity. Most times, that's when I fell!

This mechanism repeated itself so many times that, in the end, I stopped going on the skiing vacations, telling myself and others that I did not like the long lines of the ski lift, the cold and how uncomfortable my ski shoes were, etc.

It was, more or less, the same thing that happened when I drove my motorbike: exactly when I started to pick up speed, my entire nervous system tightened up. I ended up having two serious accidents—and not from speed—but from nervousness.

There is an even more subtle way that the conditioning affected me.

At the end of every year, I usually verify the year ending and set down new personal and professional objectives for the year now beginning, just like you will be invited to do in the next chapter.

In December of 1999, I was satisfied with my work, having had many successful seminars, and I felt that this was the time to make a qualitative leap. The moment had come to work with large audiences. Up to then, I had only had experience with forty or fifty people, maximum one hundred, never more. Now I felt ready to let my work reach thousands of people all at the same time! So on New Year's Day of 2000, I made that my objective for the upcoming year.

It was not even mid-January when a company called me.

A polite voice tells me that she is calling from the event planner for a large multi-national corporation. The speaker tells me about the company and that, although they don't know me personally, they had heard good things about me. In March, they were having a large convention with two thousand five hundred people. Just as I'm thinking that they want to sell me an encyclopedia or a ticket to the convention, I am asked if I would be their motivational speaker, their only speaker from outside their organization at the convention. Every one of my cells jumped for joy: two thousand five hundred people! It was exactly what I wanted and was happening so quickly! For a minute, I was not even listening to the details that I was being told so meticulously since I was so taken up by my inner celebration.

Then along came the thought killer "Go slowly. It is dangerous to go so fast. It has not been long enough." It had reawakened.

All of a sudden, my throat became dry, and I was short of breath. I hope they can't tell on the other side of the phone. The voice that had spoken, up to then, almost uninterruptedly (how did their throat not become dry?), suddenly became silent. Is it my time to talk? I have no idea of what to say. I don't even know what was being talked about. I begin to stammer, "Motivational intervention. Well, uh, what is that exactly? Well, uh, I don't know. Well, uh, what should I do?"

This is not exactly the kind of behavior one would expect from a potential convention speaker. You did not need to be in a teleconference to know what my interviewer's face looked like that moment. Maybe they were even thinking that they had reached the wrong number. Maybe she was going to hang up.

Help! What was happening? I don't know how it happened but a part of me was still able to realize what was going on. And, from that part of me, knowledge arrived asking: "What are you doing? Don't you see that it is the matrix that has been activated? It is the old 'go slowly'."

I think that, in some way, even if we deny it and say that it's time to free ourselves, we actually are attached to our conditionings. They are like old relatives, a bit grouchy, but that, in the end, we love. Maybe it's because they have been part of us for such a long time that we actually identify with them. Maybe it is because we know them and are used to them. And when we meet them, it's like finding something familiar, so much so that often we defend them and refuse to let them go.

During other times of my life, that "go slowly" was, in fact, useful, like when I went on the bicycle as a child or when, as an adolescent, I tried, heart and soul, to enter every improbable social mission. Decidedly, it would have helped during many of my sentimental relationships. But now, in this context, is it functional? But if I don't listen to his warning—just this once—would it mean that I have betrayed him? No. I am not betraying my father. It's just the opposite; my father would have wanted my success.

With this knowledge, I took a deep breath, and, with all my strength and concentration, I stopped. And, it is only then, that I began asking intelligent questions and giving sensible answers. In the second part of the conversation, the tone of my voice, my words, and my attitude changed profoundly. Now I am the person to be trusted with the job.

As Gregory Bateson reminds us, "That which exists today is only a series of messages regarding the past that we call memories. These memories can be framed and modified again at any moment."

Every time we think about the memories, we change them. With each new understanding, knowledge, development and experience, we review and update our memories because they exist only as we built them in our minds.[8]

EXPLORATION OF THE MATRIX OF TIME

Answer the following questions in your diary.

- What do you think of time?
- Is it your friend or your enemy?
- Do you have enough time?
- Where do you spend the most time—in the past, in the present or in the future?
- Are you able to easily speed up or slow down your rhythm depending on your needs?
- Is the relationship you now have with time useful? For what? What does it do for you?
- How could you change it?

THE MATRIX OF THE WORLD

We are what we think. Everything that we are is born in our thoughts. With our thoughts, we create the world.

—Buddha

---

[8] What we will see is only a part of Dr. Hall's work and has been modified to make it easier and more immediately useful. The complete Matrix Model is actually formed of content matrices (here to follow) and process matrices (intention and significance) but, in the book, they are treated separately.

After having met the world of our parents, our brothers and sisters, our grandparents and other relatives, our world gradually expands to include neighbors, friends from nursery school and vacation spots. Through toys, video games, cartoons and television, we are exposed to the world and to customs of the society in which we live. Later, at school, we learn about other worlds through history, geography, and even computer sciences, dance and science, which help us to know about other civilizations and cultures.

The matrix of the world contains information that we make into our own, our own personal understanding of the world in which we have traveled and the significance that we have given the many realities that are known and unknown.

Here are our beliefs regarding the world of work, the professional world, the world of organizations, of travel, of fashion, of sport, of philosophy, science, economics, religion and technology and so on.

Here we also find the concept that we have of God and of life, our beliefs regarding the universe, the origin of the world and of destiny.

Our beliefs of the worlds that surround us come from the sense that we gave them, and, depending on the importance that we attributed to them, we have different emotions.

THE INDIANS HAD NO WORDS TO DESCRIBE IT.

Our beliefs become reinforced and solidified by the society in which we live and by the group that we most identify with. This influences all the other parts of our matrix, including our ability.

In *The Indians have no words for it,* Wendell Johnson, an expert in semantics from the last century, cited a study done on various Native American tribes. The researchers were shocked to discover that there were no stutterers in these tribes. At the beginning, they thought that it might have been genetic but then they noted that, among the little Indian orphans who were adopted by white families, there was evidence of stuttering. They analyzed all the probable causes until they discovered that there was no word in their language to define the phenomenon of stuttering. If it did not exist in their dictionary, it did not exist in their mind either. Without an idea, a word to classify it, stuttering did not exist. In that world, stuttering was described as a temporary difficulty with words or a pause for reflection, and because these phenomena were not associated with any emotional problem, sense of shame, judgment or stress, they remained sporadic.

I ask myself what would happen if, in our world, there were no idea of failure. We would probably behave completely differently when faced with not being able to reach certain pre-established objectives. So, instead of feeling shame, dishonor or inadequacy, we would think of it as a natural part of learning or simple feedback on what did not work. In *The Matrix Model*, Michael Hall writes that, when an entire society catalogues the experience of not reaching the goals hoped for in a negative way, the concept of failure is invented.

WAR OF MEANINGS

We suffer, get angry and fight, not for things themselves, but for the meanings and consequent value that we have given them. As we will better see later, through our emotions, we feel in our body the meanings created by our mind.

History is full of human beings who have given their lives or killed to defend the significances they had of the world. But how many are willing to review or expand those meanings? The most striking example that we see still today is in the field of religion. At various times, millions of humans have fallen in war to defend their own idea of God, their own interpretation of the facts and to secure power. This type of war exists even today in worlds other than those of religion, politics or economics but also the family and work worlds. Up to what point do you feel that you must defend your ideas, your meanings?

How open are you to the ideas and convictions of others? Do you try to make the world adapt to you or are you willing to adapt to the world? Do you prefer to live in peace or to fight to be right?

In ancient times, it was thought that, beyond the boundaries of the known world, there were dragons and horrible monsters. Hence, most people were careful not to go beyond the known limits. Very few courageous explorers dared to go beyond. The same mechanism works today on the psychological level. Every one of us possesses our own precise map of the world where safe territories are drawn. They are composed of our beliefs, norms and convictions. Beyond these lands, there is danger of the unknown that our mind assumes to be monstrous.

How often do you go beyond these limits to explore other maps and other meanings? How do you compare the worlds that are different from your own? Or other cultures, races, religions, customs, ideas? How wide are your borders? How often do you feel threatened? Is the world a safe or dangerous place?

BAD MANNERS OR RESPECT?

Being in contact with more worlds, physically or virtually, and exploring more contexts helps us realize that reality actually has thousands of facets, and our point of view is only one of them. For a vegetarian like me, it is difficult to understand the typical custom of certain African tribes to offer guests of honor a drink of milk and cow's blood. I was so firm in my position that I had to work very hard to convince myself to drink at least a sip of that concoction. And yet now, after almost thirty years, I must admit that, as with everything, it was all-relative. A woman in our world who is considered overweight would be marginalized in other cultures because she is too skinny. Illegal actions in one country are encouraged in another. Removing shoes to enter a building or sitting on the ground are bad manners in one culture but a form of respect in another.

How well do you know the world of your colleagues, friends and clients? When you discover differences, do you consider them, respect them? If yes, how? According to which rules do you decide who is right and who is wrong? Is there an absolute truth?

THE EXPLORATION OF THE MATRIX OF THE WORLD

Answer the following questions in your diary.

- What do you think of life?
- How is the world?
- What worlds do you know best? In which have you navigated the least? Which ones would you like to know better?
- What do you think about other cultures, races and religions? Of those who have different opinions than yours?
- Are you interested in exploring new worlds? Which worlds would you not explore for any reason?

REPROGRAM THE MATRIX

What have you discovered traveling in the matrix? Are your beliefs useful? Do they help you live better? If not, you will find exercises to modify them in the paragraphs dedicated to the paradoxical advantage and the magic of the word.

AFRAID OF CHANGE?

Progress is impossible without change and those who are not able to change their minds cannot change anything.

—*George Bernard Shaw*

While reading these pages, have you wondered how many false and dysfunctional beliefs you have made your own? Many people are so accustomed to their own character that they are convinced that they are not capable of changing it. Most of us change only when we have no other choice.

The problem is, however, as stated by philosopher Ken Wilber, that if our potential is formed from about one hundred units (represented by vital energy, time, thought, behavior) and we use forty units to satisfy false needs from old parts of our personality, we only have sixty units left to use for our development and our evolution.

Is this what we want? Why, then, do we fear change so much?

24-HOUR ROOM SERVICE

For the nine months that we live in our mother's womb, we have twenty four hour room service. Without even asking, everything that we need is provided directly. We are warm, embraced by the amniotic liquid that rocks us and protects us, and we receive all the nutrition that we need. Then, all of a sudden, it is time to leave. Often we are not ready but we find ourselves pushed down a narrow and uncomfortable passageway that we must go through. It is not an easy time.

After having passed this nerve-wracking test, we end up in a place that, for us, is cold, too bright for our eyes which have been used to darkness, and the air that enters our lungs for the first time burns like fire. We are not even sure that we will survive or if we will be able to take care of or even nourish ourselves.

This is the first big change in our life. It was much better before! Federick Leboyer, expert in natural delivery, sustains that being born is like landing on the moon with no preparation—yet we all made it.

It's not surprising that we worry when we think about change. The belief that most of us have created is that change hurts; it's uncomfortable and painful. There is no doubt that we tend to avoid it. During birth, we are physically separated from our mother's body, so, unconsciously, change is often associated with separation or breaking.

Because of this, most people, rather than feeling the pain and experiencing the uncertainty of that separation, would prefer to remain in even a dysfunctional situation—an old job, a relationship, a habit. To throw oneself toward something new would mean to cut the umbilical cord and feel again that pain and deep fear.

Imagine what it would be like to confront change if our belief was that change is easy and fun. Or that change brings togetherness and completion. Or that change is completely safe. Or every time I change, I grow and get better. Would it be different?

What meaning do you give to change? What beliefs do you have about it? Do they encourage you to create the transformations that you desire?

CHAPTER 4

WHERE DO WE WANT TO GO?

*Try to get whatever you want or you will have
to be happy loving what you get.*

—Anonymous

Now that we have navigated in matrix and have realized
where we are from and what holds us back, it is time to
define exactly what it is that we want and where want to go.

In this chapter, we will ask questions that will help to
clarify which direction to take and to analyze the scale of
human needs and the structure of motivation. We will contact our dreams and our hopes and discover how to activate
our potentiality. We will see what stimulates us, what pushes
us to action and what sustains us when faced with difficulty.

ESTABLISH A GOAL

> *When there is a goal, even the desert becomes a road.*
>
> *—Old Tuareg saying*

At the beginning of almost any trip, it is important to establish a goal. Otherwise, we risk getting lost and never reaching our destination or wasting gasoline, time and even energy. Often, we, too, have no idea of where we are going in life. When asked the question, "What do you want from life?" our response is an expression of utter bewilderment accompanied by a phrase of the type, "I don't want to get sick or suffer. I want to be well." (Well? In what sense? What must happen for you to be well?) In effect, it's much easier to answer that way rather than to force ourselves to think about what we really want. But if we have no answer, our only hope is that someone else has one for us—and—we must have the good fortune that their solution is something that we like.

When we talk about objectives, many of us behave differently than we ever would in everyday life. It's as if, at a restaurant, when ordering, we tell the waiter, "I don't know why I'm here." Maybe those of us, who are more assertive, dare to say, "I want something good to eat." The waiter could respond, "Good in what sense? What do you like? Sweet, salty, spicy? Hot or cold? Meat or fish?" So you look at him and, after having thought a bit, tell him, "I don't want to eat fruit. Nor do I want anything like salami, make that clear. And I hope that boiled fennel isn't brought to me..."

What type of meal can you expect from a similar order? How many possibilities are there to your liking?

Having a precise destination offers a direction for the mind, a route on which to focus our attention. Once we have intentionally decided on objectives, they function as a true and real magnet for thought and potential and make our every action move toward the realization of our vision.

This mechanism works in such a way that even our perception is influenced and we begin to understand parts of reality that, earlier, we did not even take into consideration. It is a mechanism that we have all more or less experienced and that functions with every kind of objective, from the insignificant to the most important.

A BARREL FULL OF DOGS OR CARS?

About five years ago, I wanted to get a new car. After having taken various makes and models into consideration, I chose the Freelander by Land Rover. From the very moment in which I decided on the car that I wanted—even before buying it—I was upset to notice that the whole world had one—from my neighbors to my friends and even to participants in my courses. Everybody. Besides that, wherever I looked, there were articles, brochures and people who talked about this car. In that same period, Silvia, my assistant, was thinking about getting a dog. And without having told her about my experience, the same thing happened to her. So whenever we travelled together, I only saw Freelanders and her world was filled with dogs.

Richard Alpert, a former professor of psychology at Harvard, who became the famous spiritual teacher Ram Dass in the 1960s, often used an interesting example to explain this phenomenon very well. If you are hungry and walk down the street, there is no doubt that you will notice only restaurants, bars, pizzerias and grocery stores.

But if you walk on the same street with the idea of finding company for the evening, your attention will be captured by something completely different. And probably, if you pass by a bakery and are surrounded by the aroma of the delicacies just taken from the oven, when someone asks if there are any stores that sell food on that street, you would have no idea. You had not seen any. But you would know exactly how many cute girls had passed by and how many potential competitors receiving their attention you had found.

"I can't take my job any more. I can't stand following decisions that aren't mine. I feel like I'm in a cage, but if I look outside, I see only fog and it stops me from leaving. I don't really know what I want to do, and, besides, there aren't many opportunities out there, so I choose the least of all evils and try to put up with it. At the end of the day, I do have a family to support." Andrew is the manager of a large corporation. In a short time, he had an enviable career but, at the same time, he had begun to feel that he did not like what he did. He dreams of something different but, in reality, he's not at all sure what he wants. By changing, he is afraid that he will not be able to make it financially. Tall and thin, he vents his frustrations with sports. Skiing competitions and long bicycle rides seem to keep him alive. His discontent shows in the family, too. A friend of his signed him up for one of my weekend courses. When he came in, he looked spaced. "I got here spontaneously," he said jokingly. "I'm not sure if I need all this but, at least, these two days are dedicated just for me."

During the course, Andrew took the time to redefine his objectives. He identified that he would like to import Australian sport products into Europe, and, gradually, as he's talking about this project, his eyes light up. In the days after the course, he continued to think about how to put it into practice. Something snapped inside him. He remembered someone he knew that had worked in imports for years; he could help him verify the feasibility of the project. Not only that! By chance, he ran into other managers who, even with families like his, had left lucrative, but unsatisfying, jobs to try new adventures. The fact that none of them ended up in misery encouraged him.

"Why did I not meet them before?" he asked us a few months after he had quit his job and opened, with great satisfaction, his new office. "It's strange. Where were all these people a year ago? It was only after I started to clearly define my objectives that all the pieces of the puzzle began to come together."

DON'T THINK OF A WHITE ELEPHANT...

Once the goal is clearly established, our psychophysical system activates a flow of creative energy toward the realization of that goal, whether it is small or large. It's as if our goal becomes larger and multiplies around us.

"That's what happened to me, too. But there's one thing that I don't understand: I knew what I wanted before. But I did not want to make the wrong move and make my family suffer. Yet, I did not want to work in a place with so much bureaucracy and such power plays, where there was no room for free initiative. Why...?" Andrew interrupted himself without finishing the phrase, maybe because he had already answered his own question. Since the mind works principally by symbols and representations, the unconscious works hard to register the word "not" and spontaneously tends to focus on the image that comes after the "not."

Need an example? Carefully read the following, "Don't think, absolutely do not think about a white elephant." Now tell me what you thought of... Imagine what happened to Andrew when he said to himself, "I don't want to make a wrong move and make my family suffer." What was he telling his unconscious? What images and what direction was he giving?

What do you tell your unconscious? Do you spend your life thinking of a white elephant?

It is fundamental to learn to order exactly what you desire at the restaurant of life. On the contrary, we cannot be surprised by not obtaining it. Above all, if we do not clearly define a goal, how can we know if we are going in the right direction?

"Once it was clear exactly what I wanted, I moved in that direction. My biggest problem was that I did not know what I wanted for so long. I felt a sense of dissatisfaction but did not know why. And, more than that, my objectives were at odds with one another…" "Andrew smiled while remembering that period of his life.

How often do we also have conflicting objectives? We want a job that is well paid—but we want to avoid too much responsibility and overtime. We want good health—but, at the same time, we drink, smoke and fill ourselves with stress. Every one of us has many goals within ourselves, many possible paths to follow that often point in opposite directions. Which do you intend to follow? The choice is in your hands.

Does it come spontaneously to you to limit yourself from taking what life offers? Are you afraid that this approach will squash spontaneity? Do you know that it is not you who will choose the direction? It will be matrix which will do it for you and which will guide you with all the information and conditions within it. But in what direction will it push you?

A QUESTION OF N/UM

> *It's not important how strong reason screams its rules of good conduct; passion always screams louder.*
>
> —*Eramus*

"How is it possible to walk barefoot on burning coals that could have a temperature between 400 and 1400 degrees?" Andrew was decidedly worried about his feet. I could give him at least a dozen different answers.

It's been more than twenty years that I have guided people over hot coals, and I have heard this question a thousand times. In my research, I have found different theories, some of which are pseudo-scientific, others completely absurd. The one I find most interesting is that of the Kung, a remote population of Bushman from the Kalahari Desert in southern Africa. They have been practicing their ritualistic fire dance for over thousands of years. Their fire ritual involves doing incredible things: not only walking and dancing on fire but crawling on the hot coals, rubbing them down their chest and up their back while they generate the n/um or healing energy that combats illness and fosters the !kia, a powerful rascendental state.

So I decide to tell Andrew about the Kung teachings.

Throughout history, the capabilities of this tribe have fascinated various anthropologists. Perhaps one of the best stories comes from Richard Katz, professor at Harvard, who wrote in the book, *Boiling Energy*, about it. As Katz writes, along with feelings of release and liberation, !kia also brings profound feelings of pain and fear. When the potential master of n/um can face the fact that he must die to himself and feel assured that he will be born again, then he can face the fear, overcome it, and break through to the !kia state.

I have often heard Peggy Dylan, who, in the eighties, brought fire walking into the realm of personal growth, summarize, "We can walk on fire and come out unscathed if the human n/um is superior to the n/um of the fire."

Simple, no? But what does it mean?

The closest translation to the word n/um is, appropriately, energy. It means that when our energy is higher than

that of the fire, we have the force and the capability to confront it and win. In other words, to beat the fires (the challenges) of life, we must raise our inner energy (n/um) to a
higher level than that of the difficulty which we are facing
and that allows us to transform our fears into action.

"But what does it mean to raise our inner energy and
how can we do it?" Andrew seems very interested, but I'm
not sure if he's thinking of the bed of coals that he will face
in a few hours or of the red hot coals of life—or maybe both.

It comes spontaneously for me to ask him, "Think about
moments in which you felt fire burn ardently within you, so
much so that your heart beat hard and you felt such a strong
excitement that you could think of nothing else. When was
it? What was it about? Was it the fire of passion that animated you at that time?" He did not have to answer me with
words. His expression said it all.

What happens when we feel passion? What are we like?
How do we behave? Have you ever noticed that, when we are
passionate, we are not aware of the passage of time that we
find strength, capacity, good humor and we even confront
problems with a smile on our lips?

Do we not have more access to our potential in those
moments? Suddenly, all our senses are more active, our minds
are more focused and clear, and we are more creative, alive,
more capable of finding solutions and even more beautiful.
"Yes, it's almost a mysterious force. But exactly how does it
work?" Andrew wants to know.

LOVE IN ACTION

Passion is nothing more than love in action. Thousands
of writings have been offered on the force and power of love
throughout history. When we put our capacity to love in
action, it becomes an incredible driving force.

Unfortunately, in our society, the concept of passion is automatically associated with romantic love or sex and rarely leaves room for other meanings.

There is nothing wrong with feeling passion for another person, but, having to resort to the stimulus of a love affair to take advantage of this state of mind, is very limiting. In addition, by expecting a thousand things of our significant other and making them responsible for our happiness is the best way to ruin a relationship.

"That's what was happening to my marriage. I no longer had passion for life and I blamed my relationship. I threw myself into sports but even that was not enough. Sometimes I thought, that maybe, a new partner would make me feel alive. In the past that's what I did, but it did not work for long. I don't think that's the solution. The secret is elsewhere." Andrew is very interested in this topic.

Our capacity to ignite the flame of love is, in fact, much broader. We can extend our love to life in general, to nature, to animals, to a dream, to a cause or to an ideal.

What makes your heart race? What does your love burn for? Discovering this means finding an inexhaustible energy to apply to your life. It means being able to be eternally in love. It means discovering the key to self-motivation.

WHAT MOTIVATES A PERSON TO DO WHAT THEY DO?

Writing, reading, studying and giving courses are part of what I love to do. No one needs to motivate me to do this. I am passionate about them even when I am not successful or when I'm tired and in need of rest. I don't consider it work, so much so, that, even while on vacation, I write and study regularly. Maybe it's natural to be drawn to do the things we love? In these cases, we don't need continuous pressure to keep our motivation high.

Have you ever asked yourself what motivates people to do what they do? What pushes them to make sacrifices and do unimaginable hard work?

Think about sports persons who train continuously, inventors, scientists, businessmen or simple parents who pass sleepless nights. They dedicate every minute of their life to something or someone. Think about people who have contributed to changing the world like Mahatma Gandhi, Mother Teresa of Calcutta, Nelson Mandela and many others—famous or not. Do you think their journey was easy with no difficulties or distractions? Do you think they were never afraid or discouraged? That they never felt inadequate? From their biographies, we learn that it was not like that. In general, the more lofty the goal, the more are the obstacles. And yet, they succeeded. And they are human beings just like us. The difference is that they put their power of love into action and did not stop believing in their dream. It was the intensity of that love that pushed them to develop the necessary capacities to overcome fear, obstacles and distractions. To come upon obstacles is normal; it's part of the game.

"It's true; when you face so many obstacles, it's not easy…. They almost suffocate your passion. You think, 'So what if I'm disappointed.'" Andrew whispers, as if speaking to himself.

Of course, it's not easy. But the difference between those who achieve their vision and those who do not, does not depend on the obstacles encountered. It is the way the obstacles are dealt with that makes the difference. Having worked with thousands of people, I've noticed that those who best achieve their dreams, even against every probability of success, are those who worry least about failure. They are the people who are convinced that, at least, they will have learned something new. In this way, they enjoy the journey toward their goal as much as their arrival to the finish line.

Three thousand years ago, Patanjali, the most studious of the Raja Yoga, wrote, "When you are inspired by great motivations and extraordinary projects, your mind transcends all limits, your conscious expands in every direction and you find yourself in a new, great and fantastic universe. Dormant forces, faculties and talents wake up and you discover yourself as a person greater than you ever would have imagined."

...AND NEED FOR SELF-REALIZATION

Self-realized people have so much to teach us that sometimes they seem like they are human beings of a different species.

—Abraham Maslow

When we speak of awakening our own capacities, teachings of modern psychology confirm the antique wisdom of tribal Africa. To help you to completely understand the importance and significance of self- realization, allow me to dwell on the events that brought psychological research toward this direction.

Around the middle of the last century in America, there was a true revolution in the field of the human psyche. Until then, psychology was exclusively interested in studying cures for mental illnesses and was concentrated on obscure parts of the human being, instincts and negative drives. For the first time, around 1940, with the outbreak of World War II, certain psychologists decided to focus on the bright side of humans and on their tendency toward evolution. Research finally began to take an interest in healthy, sane people and to help them live better.

With this was born the Human Potential Movement, to which great experts, such as father of Gestalt[9]Fritz Perls and family therapist Virginia Satir, adhered. All these brilliant minds had a deep passion for developing the human potential and had a clear goal: to create a scientific basis that could help people improve and be happier.

In his research, Maslow noted that some people were more productive, healthier, more able to offer their contribution and more capable of making a difference in the world. He started calling these people *self-actualizers* or self-realized. Quickly he discovered that they were only two per cent of the population. "Why weren't the others? What were the prerequisites for self-realization? What motivates us?" Maslow wondered.

So, it was in 1954, in his book *Motivation and Personality* that he exhibited the first model of human motivation and design, that which became known as the famous pyramid of needs. Over time, the work of Maslow has remained a solid base in the area of personal development, so much so that it is still followed by current psychologists. What are human needs? And how do we take them into account as we try to establish our goals?

THE PYRAMID OF NEEDS

While studying the behavior of chimpanzees, Maslow noted that certain needs seemed stronger than others.

For example, we may believe that sex is an important need, but would it be the first thing you would need if you had nothing to eat?

---

[9] Branch of psychology born at the beginning of the twentieth century in Germany and later transferred to the U.S, which sustains that the mind works in a holistic manner.

Between hunger and thirst, which is more important? It seems that it is thirst because you can resist eating longer than you can drinking. And between thirst and the need to breathe? Again, the second is more important because we can be without drink longer because we need oxygen to live. This is more or less the idea at the base of the hierarchy of need proposed by Maslow, at least regarding the first levels.

—Abraham Maslow: *The Hierarchy of Needs*, 1954.

According to this theory, in fact, human needs are divided into five overlapping levels that together form a pyramid as you can see in the design below.

At the base of the pyramid, there are physiological needs such as oxygen, water and food. This category also includes the need to sleep, to eliminate toxins (sweat, feces, urine), the need to avoid pain and to engage in sexual activity. At this level, our needs are not very different from those of animals.

When these needs are met, we step up a level and find the need for order, safety, stability and protection.

It is here that we position many of our anxieties, and it is because of this that many aspire to the guarantee of a permanent job and choose a safe area in which to live. To satisfy this type of need, companies that provide security doors and surveillance systems have risen, as have those of insurance and pension funds. Even at this level, we are not very different from animals, which don't worry about their pension but do seek safe places in which to retreat. The third level is about social needs: affection and identification. The same need is felt in many animals. Those most evolved, in fact, seek out their herd and live in an organized society. It is this level that pushes us toward marriage, to have children and to find friends. It is for this that we tend to want to be part of a group or community. We enroll in clubs; we create volleyball and soccer teams. This sense of belonging is often a large part of what we look for in a career.

Gradually, as we interact with others, our need for esteem, appreciation, recognition and success emerges. Here we are at the fourth level. If you think that we behave differently than the animal world at this level, you are mistaken. Have you ever observed battles to become leader of the pack in wild species or watched a pet wait for the caress of its owner? At this level, we seek esteem from external sources: status symbols, fame, glory, and reputation. Self-esteem and love for ourselves, on the other hand, provide the base for the fifth level that finally differentiates us from animals: the need for self-realization.

All our needs up to the fourth level are guided by deficiencies. As soon as we lack food, safety, a relationship or appreciation, we begin to feel the need so much so that its absence is painful. So we do everything we can to placate our need. But, once this need is satisfied and we have everything that we need, after a brief period of happiness, we don't feel anything again. That which motivated us earlier, once acquired, no longer has importance, that is, until we lose something (money, work, friends, partner or recognition) and again feel the overwhelming need. And so forth, every need keeps us busy until we gratify it. Then, once satisfied, needs from the next level emerge.

Up until the fourth level, it is not about growing and improving; it is about survival needs, the same that the most intelligent animals feel. The idea here is not evolution but only the conservation of the species and even love and esteem are required to achieve this.

The self-realization level is completely different, so much so that many diagrams show it separate from the other levels. To explain this, Maslow used various definitions: the need of being and the motivator for growth. This is in contrast to the names given at other levels: the need for survival and necessity.

The push toward self-realization is the instinctive need of human beings to expand and maximize their abilities and to work toward becoming the best that they can. Rogers defined this as the need to become all that we can: completely functional people. It is the little voice that tells us to try to proceed the best way possible, to want to give our contribution to the world. It is a journey toward improvement that will never end because, as long as we live, there is always room for growth. This level also includes everything that helps us evolve, to discover our own uniqueness and to give life to spiritual qualities, to realize our own identity and our reason for living. The needs of being can be varied: cognitive needs of learning and comprehension, beauty, order and, finally, the realization of your own potential.

The push toward self-fulfillment can present itself in many different forms and can take different forms such as art, science, literature, dance, music, math, spirituality, love of Earth and animals and service to others depending on the individual's predisposition and capabilities. In what way does your push toward self- realization present itself? What are your capabilities and passions?

Maslow sustained that individual capacities are not only latent potentiality but are also needs to satisfy, true and real pushes to express ourselves.

A SURE WAY TO FRUSTRATION

All this time, Andrew was silent. "The reason I had to work so hard to give up my job was safety. If I analyze my matrix, I still hear my father's voice telling me enjoyment and work don't go together. According to him, work was the way to earn the most money possible and to provide safety in old age. 'It does not matter that you're not passionate about your work; passion is for your free time,' he always told me. And I followed his example. My passion was sport, but I never thought about making it into a job. In this sense, I think I realized a part of myself, but do we all have the possibility to fulfill our 'self'?? Isn't that something just for the more fortunate?" he asked looking at me thoughtfully.

Maslow defined self-realized people not as people to whom something had been added but as individuals from whom nothing had been taken, to whom nothing had inhibited their potentiality. This means that every individual has an innate tendency to develop their own potential and become complete. The problem is that while the most basic needs are physiological and, if not met, scream their discomfort, the push toward self-realization comes from the heart, is infinitely more subtle, and, because of this, easier to deny and suppress. In most cases, we go through life at the survival level, in search of food, rest, fun, sex, safety, affection and esteem. We decide to research change only when one of the necessary elements for survival is taken away. Depending on the contents of our matrix, we can more strongly feel our needs at a certain level. For example, if, as children, we suffered hunger, or lived through war or suffered a strong affective loss, we risk remaining stuck in that level and leaving all our objectives there.

"I'm the first of four brothers. My father worked in a factory and my mother was a seamstress working from home. Money was always tight. For my father, to have a son with a secure position with a good salary was a dream come true. I think I confused self-realization with moneymaking for many years. I felt this push and applied it to earning money, to my career. But it was never enough. No matter how much I made, I was never satisfied. Now I understand why!" Andrew exclaimed, as if it were obvious.

What we learn about our needs is healthy, and when we satisfy a need of the lowest level, it is fulfilled (e.g. after a good meal, we are no longer hungry). This is how we learn to control our most basic needs. In this way, even when the needs are reactivated by life's events, we don't experience strong deficiency.

But, if the beliefs in our matrix are toxic, if we incorrectly learn about our needs, we will end up giving them distorted significances, and, like Andrew, we replace self-realization with a lesser need. The problem is that, contrary to other needs, self-realization is never exhausted; there is never enough. If we put another need in its place and try to fulfill ourselves this way, it will never work. We will never feel as though we have enough money, enough affection, enough recognition, safety, food, etc.

WHICH NEEDS DO WE SATISFY?

Surely it's difficult to think of improving and discovering new things when we don't have food or our life is in danger, but Gandhi, Mandela, Mother Teresa, Viktor Frankl, and Martin Luther King and many others are clear examples of the fact that it is possible. With their lives, they demonstrated that we can rise above the lower needs until we transcend them.

It's only a question of choice, and that decision, unlike what happens to animals, is within our power zone. At what level do we choose to live? What meanings do we choose to give to our needs? All you have to do is turn on the television, look at the newspaper or look at advertising billboards to realize how much emphasis is placed on satisfying the lowest level of needs in current society. It's not surprising, given that our economy lives by this. But is this all there is to life? When you think of your vision, of your goals, ask yourself which are the needs that will be met? What level are they from? How do you choose to satisfy your needs?

"We are about to design the map of our goals. I want a new house, but it is only at the second or third level, stability and protection. You don't think that's a good idea? You think I should only want things that belong to the last level?" Lisa, the companion of Andrew, seemed confused. There's something strange in her behavior. I can't quite understand if it's just that she's timid or if it's something else. She pushed Andrew to come to the course and just now decided to work on herself as well almost a year later.

"Whatever your goals are, don't judge them; that is not the reason for these questions. It is perfectly normal to have needs and to want to satisfy them," I quickly answered. "Don't misunderstand; I never thought that some goals were better than others..."

Maslow said that mostly we must be "good animals" because our needs are not mean or negative on their own. They are only nudges that we feel and that, when handled in the correct way, help us to make the necessary adjustments to live better and to have success. Both groups of needs, the inferior and the superior, are valid and important because they work together in a systemic manner.

As we learn to adequately satisfy our lower level needs, they are exhausted and we are gradually pushed to the superior levels until the need of self-realization emerges. It is important to not give too much importance to any given meaning and to stop using substitutes and false gratifications.

MUST I GIVE AWAY MY FERRARI?

In certain Asian disciplines, the practice of separation from all that is transitory is recommended, including all material goods. At one class, a participant actually asked, "Does that mean that I have to give away my new Ferrari?" No, you do not have to give up your Ferrari, and, if a Ferrari is among your goals, that is fine. Whatever object, whatever need, be it healthy or toxic, depends on the meaning that we give it.

When we make goals for ourselves, it is important to take stock of the true value they have for us, why they have such significance, what the particular goal means to us and what kind of need it satisfies. This work of awareness will help us to be honest with ourselves and allow us to free ourselves from false goals. It is an invitation to analyze and reflect on our feelings and on the significance that we want to give to our existence.

Do we want to live for the more elevated human needs of beauty, order, truth, justice, love, excellence, uniqueness and fulfillment, or is our development blocked by a particular need? Since we are humans, we cannot continue to live only at the lowest level of needs without becoming damaged. We are programmed to continue to open ourselves so we can transcend the lowest needs and begin to realize the potential of the higher needs.

In the end, even self-realization is a biological need, an innate process of development that is in us and which guides us to become completely human, completely alive and which gives more significance to our lives.

THE MEANING OF LIFE

> *We all have a spiritual goal, a mission that we follow without knowing it. In the moment in which we bring it completely to our conscious, our life can take off.*
>
> —*James Redfield*

"So to achieve self-realization does not mean to simply clarify one's own objectives, but to also find the reason, the mission of our life?" Andrew smiled, maybe the word mission reminded him if his old corporation. But if having a mission is so important for the entrepreneurial world, why should not it be for every single individual?

A study done in France a few years ago showed that 89 percent of people suffer from the lack of a deep reason to live. Most of the people interviewed were not interested in philosophizing about the significance of existence in general, but that which they felt a great need to understand was the reason for their own life. This research simply confirms what we have always known: a human being needs a reason to live.

Every organ in our body has a very precise function, as does every gear in a machine, every aspect of nature and every part of life. Everything in the universe has a reason. Why shouldn't we humans?

It's a concept as old as the Earth that we find in both Eastern and Western cultures. The reason for living is like a mission, a call similar to a vocation that guides and motivates us. It is something that is at the base of our creativity and our desire to know but also an anchor to grab on to when everything around us falters. When we listen to this calling, we understand what our position in life is. It's as if something inside us is about to be fulfilled.

If, however, there is no reason to live, we drift; we risk not knowing who we are. We end up marrying the wrong person, accepting the wrong job and so on. Until one day, we wake up—maybe at sixty or eighty years old—and we realize that our life is not working. Why don't we try to find out sooner?

Before we even ask where we want to go, we must ask who we want to be. What is guiding you? What meaning do you want to give to your existence? What legacy do you want to leave from your journey on Earth?

"It's not easy to answer these questions," Andrew laments.

If it seems difficult to give an answer, it is because there is more than one trap into which it is easy to fall.

A Unique Way to Contribute

The first thing we think is why some callings are for some people only: poets, musicians, scientists, men and women of the cloth. However, it's not like that at all. Every one of us has a role, a unique way to contribute to the world. It does not have to be a grand thing, as long as it is authentic and comes from your true self.

Rose is an elderly Thai woman who owns a small restaurant at the center of the island of Phuket. It is definitely not a luxurious place and not even easy to find because there are no signs, and, to get there, you must get in through the back of a Japanese restaurant. Since she was a child, Rose, small and chubby, had a great passion for food and a great dream—to open a restaurant. Her parents were poor immigrants from Penang in Malaysia. Rose had to put her dream aside and start to work hard. Things got a bit better when she was hired by a bank, but with so many relatives, the money was never enough and she worked there for over thirty years. At almost sixty years old, with her very little lifetime savings and a lot of courage, she finally opened her small restaurant. The atmosphere is that of old Indo-china, and the food is delicious and unique, so much so that they say even the royal family has sent for certain dishes. I have never known anyone who left there unhappy. Every friend I have brought there was enthusiastic. Within a short amount of time, the restaurant had many clients. In every plate, in every entrée, you feel the love and dedication of this small woman, who, while she takes orders, smiles warmly through her beautiful eyes. Each of her gestures and every particular of the restaurant speak of her life's goal—to nourish people and make them feel good.

"I get up at four every morning and go to the market," she says. "When I get back, I start to cook, clean the vegetables, the fish and prepare the meat. At eleven, I open the restaurant and stay there until midnight. When I close, I get everything back in order and at about one at night, I go to bed. For more than ten years, I have been open 365 days a year. A lot of people think I'm crazy and that, at my age, I should not be working so hard. But I am happy. I love to stay and talk to people. It's nice to see them arrive from all parts of the world, leave and come back again. I have never travelled, but every time my clients go back to their countries, it seems as if I travel with them. It makes me happy to know that most of the people are more than clients; they have become friends." As she says these words, her face lights up and she smiles shaking her head like a typical old Asian.

Do you think it's always been easy for Rose? Certainly not. I went to visit her a few days after the tsunami in December of 2004. Rose lost many people close to her, and, because all the tourists had left the island, for a whole season, she had barely any clients. Did this make her give up? Certainly not. Her dream went on.

* * *

"In the books and in the courses, when we speak of mission, up to now we have always heard about famous people. I thought only the fortunate had a goal in life. So it's not like that?" Andrew seemed as surprised as if he had heard that the Earth was square.

If we speak more often of Mozart, Einstein or Edison, it's only because everybody knows what they did and because it's easier to use them as an example rather than to use Rose. But, if we pay attention to people like Rose who, to quote Coelho, ". . . are living their personal legend," there are more than we could imagine. And when we meet them, we realize why their work somehow touches our lives.

BEYOND HIS OWN SKIN

We are social beings and our behavior, our work and our choices influence other people. The reason for living goes "beyond one's own skin"—goes beyond our personal or family interests and becomes beneficial for the world. To create personal goals, with the objective that they go beyond ourselves, calls on our innate ability to contribute and to be helpful. This makes the effect even more powerful.

To know our personal mission gives another perspective to our objectives. Mostly, it makes us do a quality control check of what we want. Then it helps us check to see if the means and strategies that we are using to get there are aligned with who we are and who we want to be. It makes us focus on the reason that those objectives are so important to us, as you will see in the exercises at the end of this chapter.

"What does it exactly mean when you say give a new perspective to our objectives?" asks Andrew.

Seven years ago, when Nicola and I had decided to live in the Far East for four months a year, we found that we had to resolve two issues—our visa and our finances. These four months, in fact, would have given us the possibility of deep meditation and time to dedicate to our studies and introspection, but it meant renouncing a large part of our work—and our earnings.

But, quite quickly, we discovered that, right where we were going to live, on the island of Phuket, there were important law offices that were looking for consultants in international law, and Nicola, who was an international lawyer, was a perfect candidate. I, on the other hand, could use my experience and credentials as a director of fashion shows and set photography, since the world of fashion was growing quickly there. It would be a good salary for us both, easy and, most probably, would have resolved the problem of our visa.

In the end, it would be occasional consulting work and would leave us enough free time to study and achieve our goal of living on the island for part of the year. But how much of it was aligned with our personal mission?

Neither Nicola nor I had the slightest doubt or a minimum of regret of not having made that choice. It was not because it was bad in and of itself but because it did not express, in any way, who we were. We found other solutions for the visa and work, solutions that we had to create, certainly less easy, but that were part of who we want to be and were in line with our reason for living. That, for example, is how the course "Spirituality, Vitality and Well-being" was born and through which many people have found great benefit in their lives.

When we align the objectives and the means that we use for our own personal mission, it's like uniting pieces of a puzzle. All the parts of our life are finally in the right place. Let's not limit ourselves to believing that all of this is reserved for elite scientists, teachers or missionaries. Whatever work or action we take, can, as in the case of Rose, be supported by our mission.

* * *

Another common error is to think that having a mission that contributes to the world, you must have extraordinary talents—which we don't have. Musicians know how to play; painters know how to paint. "And me? I have no such particular talent," you may respond.

It is not true! Often we have no idea of what our talents are just because we have never had reason to discover them. As we've seen in earlier chapters, in general, we are so busy with everyday things that we don't allow ourselves the time to develop our capabilities or to stop and listen to possible callings. By doing this, our potential remains hidden in our unconscious and begins to emerge only when we put aside rationality and give it permission to come out of its cage of limitations—that we have constructed. Then we can return to dreaming.

How long has it been since you have dreamt?

DISCOVER THE PURPOSE OF YOUR LIFE[10]

Step 1 – Complete the following lists.
(a). Ten things you want more of in your life.

_____

_____

_____

_____

(b). Ten things that you would most like to see happen on this planet.

_____

_____

_____

_____

(c). Ten things that make you special.

_____

_____

_____

_____

(d). Ten things that you know how to do and that you like to do (they can be abilities or qualities).

_____

_____

_____

_____

---

[10] From The Life Coach Academy, Australia.

Where Do We Want to Go?

Step 2 – For each list, decide your priorities. Identify the number one priority and put an asterisk beside it.

Step 3 – Complete the following phrases.
I, (your name) intend (first priority from question 4) using my (first priority of question 3) to achieve (first priority of question 2) and also obtain (first priority of question 1).

Align Your Purpose for Living with Your Objectives[11]

In the following paragraphs, you will complete a true and real map of objectives. In the meantime, think of your main objectives, of what you want in life and ask yourself: "Why is this important to me?"

Write the answer in your diary, and then ask yourself again (this time referring to the answer you just gave): And why is this important for me? Why does this have such significance? Is there something more important? This objective is important to you for many reasons. Why are these reasons important to you? What is the importance of possessing or becoming this? And when you completely obtain this result in the way you want it, is there anything else that is even more important?

(Keep going until you discover and identify all the superior values that sustain your objectives.)

Is this important for you? Then welcome the pleasant sensations that come from these meanings and remain a while with these superior level feelings. Do you like it?

Let these feelings grow, and they will intensify as you accept them and realize that this is part of your mission, of who you really are...right? Appreciate this knowledge.

---

[11] Liberally taken from APG Manual of Neuro-Semantics.

Here is an example to give you an idea of how this works, this is an extract of when I did the exercise with myself:

Objective: I want to write a book. Q: Why is that important for you?

A: So I can give to others my experiences and tell them how I learned the hard way.

Q: And why is that important for you?

A: So I can leave something to the world, a seed that can help others live better.

Q: What importance does this result have?

A: It will help people to live to the fullest of their potential, to love more, to fulfill themselves, to be happier, to contribute to the world.

Q: Is this important for you?

A: Yes.

Q: Well, welcome the pleasant feelings that are invited from these meanings and stay for a while with these superior level sensations. Do you like it?

A: Yes.

Q: Let these sensations grow, and they will intensify while you accept and acknowledge that this is part of your mission, of who you really are…right?

A: Yes.

Appreciate this knowledge. Now it's your turn!

LET'S DREAM AGAIN

If you can dream it, you can do it.

—*Walt Disney*

It is a frigid winter morning in Auschwitz and the day begins like any other: the alarm before dawn, the long silent march in the snow, the back-breaking work, the hunger that afflicts the body. Viktor Frankl is exhausted; so exhausted by fever and sickness that he can no longer march and falls to the ground. This can mean the end for him and he knows it. In these cases, the guards of the lager, after having repeatedly hit you to get up, will kill you. But, in that moment, Viktor thinks of his dream: to return home and conduct a new kind of psychotherapy based on the meaning of life. While he is kneeling there in the snow, he imagines himself in the future before thousands of people speaking of the value of dreams, of the importance of researching the purpose of your own life and telling how all that helped him survive this terrible adventure.

While he dreamed open-eyed, Viktor felt his strength gradually return. Just before the guard came close, he was able to stand up and reach the building where he lived and save himself.

This story was told by Viktor Frankl during a worldwide convention on psychotherapy some ten years after his experience in a concentration camp. The thousands of people present were so struck and moved that they came to their feet and applauded. Before their eyes, Frankl demonstrated exactly the scene that he dreamed of years before that gave him the hope and the strength to survive.

I CANNOT DREAM.

Do you have a dream that is so strong that it influences the way in which you live minute by minute? What are your dreams? What do you want to happen in your future?

"I can't dream. I have no big project to achieve or any particular capacities. What can I do?" asked Lisa. Her friends described her as "a good girl." She met Andrew in college, and, after she graduated, worked as a clerk for a few years. Then, with the birth of her second child, she decided to dedicate herself to the family. "Andrew already had a career," she used to say, almost as an excuse for the decision she had made. Now, at forty and with four children who were growing up and no longer needed her constant presence, she felt a bit disoriented. "The only thing I want is that the family is always fine," she says.

"Good, and for yourself? What are your dreams?" I ask her. Silence.

Unfortunately, for many of us, we were told to stop dreaming from the time we were children, and we learned to remain grounded as much as possible. We got in the habit of meeting our material needs as if the emotional ones had no importance. It's not surprising that, after many years of this kind of training, changing habits won't be easy. To dream is a completely natural activity of the human soul that, with time, we unlearned. To begin to do it again requires work and tenacity. At the beginning, you may not feel anything at all—no interior flame, no passion and no enthusiasm. But it is by dreaming with our eyes open that our objectives are born. And it is by dreaming that the forces toward self-realization and our contribution to the world start to become clear. A dream is the product of the emotional brain, of the intuitive part, of the visionary. If we don't leave space for that part, if we censure it because of fear that it will take us too far from reality, we will never access our potentiality and we will lose our essence. Renounce your dreams and you renounce living. Dreams express our deepest values, that which we believe in and tell who we are.

"Maybe it's because of this, and because I did not believe in my possibilities that I unlearned how to dream and why I am often annoyed and become depressed easily," Lisa looked at Andrew who nods, "That's right." "I was a classic example," answered Andrew with a low tone as if he were talking to himself, "For many years, I told myself that changing jobs was impossible. Every day my energy dwindled and I was more tired and nervous. I could not see any opportunities because I did not give myself permission to dream. As soon as I did begin to dream though, I got the necessary strength to put new possibilities into motion." He stopped a moment and then, almost, hesitantly, added, "Now I earn a bit less than before, but we still have everything that we need. What I lost financially, I abundantly earned in well-being and satisfaction."

Andrew is a new person, very happy with his decision and would never turn back.

Even if we have a dream, often we renounce following it. Maybe we partially reshape it, at least so we think. We cut a little bit here and there. We trade off a bit for money, another bit for security, and another to be loved and accepted. We hide behind a thousand excuses. Sometimes we accuse others: It's their fault that we ended up like this. In some cases, we play the role of the victim without choice and decide that this is life. But it is not. This is death, a slow but progressive death of our soul.

Do you have the courage to live your dreams?

CHAPTER 5

BUILDING THE VISION

Your vision becomes clear only when you can see into your heart. He who looks outside himself dreams; he who looks within himself awakens.

—*Carl Gustav Jung*

Every one spoke of him. Apparently, he was the most powerful shaman in the area. We had arrived in Cambodia a few days earlier and all our research seemed to point in the same direction. We absolutely wanted to meet this man; he had so much to teach. But how could we do it? It was not easy to get close to him and, usually, he didn't work with foreigners. Fortunately, we remembered Don, who participated in our courses in Thailand and had lived quite a few years in Cambodia. We hoped that he still had the same phone number and hadn't gone back to America in the meantime. We had good luck. Don still lived in Southeast Asia and told us how we could contact Chann, a Cambodian friend of his who knew the medicine man we wanted to meet.

We meet with Chann just outside Siem Rap and he offered to be our guide. With his help, we soon contacted the famous healer who agreed to meet with us. Bingo! Not even twenty-four hours later, we were on a broken-down motor-bike, following Chann, down a kind of jungle path. The ride on the path was difficult (maybe it was a metaphor for life?): the road had recently been cut through lush vegetation, had holes and roots everywhere and was such an obstacle course that we often had to stop. It was two in the afternoon and was infernally hot. Besides that, there were many live mines left by the Pol Pot army still underground. They could have been anywhere. It was better not to think about it. Finally, we arrived at our destination. The scene before us was—strange. In the middle of the forest, there was an opening with large wooden stilts. A hundred or so people were seated around something that I couldn't see but, based on their behavior, must have been sacred. We parked what was left of the motorbike and walked closer. The strange object was a car! Why? And, more than anything, how did it ever get there?

Very soon, I had the answer, at least to my first question. The car was an offering from an important person who the shaman had healed years ago. Obviously, it had never been used. Neither the medicine man nor anyone in his family knew how to drive. And what sense would it make to know how to drive in a place where there were no roads? This is how the car became a trophy, the symbol of the healer's power. This is why it was worshipped by his followers. We got in line with about another seventy people. Considering what time it was, we were afraid that we would be spending the night there, but, after a very short time, the shaman called us. As soon as we entered the hut, we were overcome by a strong aroma of incense and our eyes had trouble getting used to the darkness. The room was full of squatting people and was lit only by a few candles.

The famous healer was a middle-aged man, not very tall, with a sweet smile. He wore a sarong around his waist and had tattoos all over his torso. Our interpreter told us that the tattoos were of sacred designs and writings. We were asked why we were there but, mostly, what our objectives in life were. Each one of us answered while the man listened carefully and traced hieroglyphics on a red cloth handkerchief. "He is writing your objectives," Chann explained, "then the handkerchief will be blessed, and you will have to always carry it with you. Through this handkerchief, all your power will be awakened and help you realize your dreams."

Then the healer had us sit before him and asked us to stick out our tongue. I obeyed, even if my mind was lost in a thousand conjectures. What happened next, I remembered for the rest of my life. The shaman took a wooden stick and, one by one, he wrote our objectives on our tongues! "Now you even have your objectives written on you, so, from now on, your every word will be directed toward that which you desire," Chann translated.

It may be a coincidence, but everything I asked for on that occasion four years ago has come true. And, at the same time, the same has happened for Nicola and the friend who was with us.

The only drawback is that the wooden stick that was used to write on our tongues was the same that was used to write on other dozens of people present that day and in the preceding days and months—and was never washed.

ONLY THREE PERCENT...

To dream, create and imagine: do these verbs describe what we are doing? This is what Gary Hamel, professor of strategic and international management at the London

Business School, asks in his book *Leader of the Revolution*. Are you ready to set goals and lay the foundation for your future?

A few years ago, Gail Mathews, psychology professor at the Dominican University of California, conducted a study of the realization of objectives involving over two hundred participants from various social backgrounds from countries all over the world.

The volunteers were divided into five groups. The first group was asked to think only of their objectives while the second was asked to write them. The third, in addition to writing them, was asked to make a plan of action. The fourth group had to also share their objectives and plan of action with a support group. Finally, the last group had to also meet with their support group weekly and report their progress.

Who do you think reached their dreams best?

At this point, we all think it's easy to guess. "It's certainly not the first group," Andrew answered with a smile. "Probably it is the fifth that had the most success, followed by the fourth, then the third and so on."

Exactly! The study clearly proved that taking the time to examine and write your objectives in a detailed manner makes a big difference.

Matthews also demonstrated that if we share our dreams with a friend or a support group and meet with them regularly to report our progress, we have even more possibility of success. (In the following pages, in fact, we will be guided through these and other steps.)

But how many people possess a complete map of their aspirations? Unfortunately, there are very few.

"If it works so well, why do so few do it? Why don't more people do this simple exercise on themselves?" Lisa asked looking confused. Studies had shown that the people who defined and wrote down their objectives for life had much more success than those who did not. Yet, less than three per cent of the population possessed a complete map of their aspirations! "You'd have to ask them!" But I realized that Lisa expected something more. And she was not the only one. Andrew and the others were looking at me waiting for some kind of explanation. I thought about earlier days, when I was a model and even I did not do that kind of exercise. Then I thought of the time when someone spoke to me of these practices, but I did not really think about them much. I considered them a waste of time. Then during my travels, I began to have more contact with the practices and to study them. As I was navigating my thoughts, I realized that there are at least forty pairs of eyes staring at me, waiting.

"Why does only three percent of the population work at clarifying and writing down their own objectives? Maybe no one ever taught them. Maybe they only superficially heard about it and did not really trust it, as if it might even damage them in some way. Maybe some did not understand the importance of it and took it lightly. Maybe some found it easier to continue as they were and complain and blame others rather than assuming responsibility for their own life. Maybe some were afraid to have to pay too high a price to have success and to be happy. Maybe some were afraid of change."

Over the years, I think I have lived alternately through all these stages. But in this moment the better question is another: do you want to be part of that small percentage that writes your own objectives and reaches them or do you want to be part of the majority who does not?

The moment has arrived to transform your dreams into real and true objectives and to prepare the map of your vision. Once that is done, it will be like owning a detailed plan or a GPS that will help you arrive at your destination. In any moment, we can easily understand if our moods and our actions are in line with our objectives and, if they are not and you find yourself lost, you can always correct your route.

THE MAP OF YOUR FUTURE

What you are about to do is a very powerful exercise and should not be underestimated.

While I was moving the last time, I happened to find a map that I had made during the summer of 2001. I was single then and lived in an apartment in the center of Bologna, Italy. My vision was to have a house in the country with many friends, a sentimental relationship with a person with whom I could share my life and travel around the world—but also courses, seeing that, for me, giving courses is not just work but a real philosophy of life, a way of being and an important part of my daily life. In addition, I dreamed of being able to put my experiences into writing and to publish a book. Looking at that old map brought me to tears; it was exactly the life that I wanted in the minimum of details.

In one corner of the map, I had designed a small island with a sun and palm trees. At that time, I was not sure why I had done that; I thought it simply referred to my love of the tropics. Those who know me know, as I have already mentioned, that Nicola and I, along with some friends and part of the Bless You! staff, spend about four months on an island in Thailand, and another 2 in Bali. From both our homes there we can see the sun and palm trees, exactly like on the map. Evidently, my subconscious knew much better than I the significance of that small design.

It took almost five years before everything was accomplished. Some things, like the relationship, Thailand and the courses together with my companion happened quickly; others, like the house in the country and the book required more time and a lot of energy. But everything became a reality in every single detail!

And, like with me, the same magic has happened to many participants in our courses.

CREATE YOUR MAP

All things that are important and lasting start in the imagination and later find a way to become a reality. Imagination is more important than knowledge.

—Albert Einstein

For this exercise, you will need a couple of hours. You don't have to finish it all in the same day though; you can work on it again at a later time. Sometimes objectives require time to germinate, and it is common to want to touch up your map after a couple of days. The important thing is that, while you are making your map, you are focused and don't have external interferences. Nice background music and a "Do Not Disturb" sign on the door will help, too. Take a piece of paper (better yet a piece of poster board) and some markers and put them in front of you. If possible, do this while sitting on the floor. You might feel silly but this will help you return to your childhood and access your creativity and your capacity to dream of that time. Imagine six months, one year, five years from now…be sure to take into consideration all aspects of your life. Where do you want to live? In what environment do you want to be? What job do you want? What unique gift will you leave the world? What do you want as the purpose of your life?

There are two main ways to make the map of your life. In the colored insert, you can see some examples. Choose the one you prefer.

For example, you can draw a large circle at the center of your paper and divide it into pieces until you have a wheel with spokes. In each section, give a name to a part of life: work, career, family, health, finances, friends, spirituality, personal growth, hobbies, studies, entertainment, free time, volunteerism, relationships…. Then start to fill each section with your goals in that area. The advantage of this technique is that the weight given to each part of life is immediately visible.

Another technique that I, personally, often use is that of drawing a large sun at the center of which you put your name, or, better yet, put a picture of yourself. It is you at the center of your universe. Many rays branch out from the sun and each is a word representing a goal, a part of your life that you want to improve. Linked to the main branches you will draw second- and third-level branches that contain details or various aspect of the goals of the main branch. This again will be of great help because the brain works by *association* and it tends to naturally link two (or more) things together.

I invented this special technique combining the well known Tony Buzan's mind mapping with the traditional vision board exercise. Mind mapping is a powerful graphic technique which provides a universal key to unlock the potential of the brain. It harnesses the full range of cortical skills—word, image, number, logic, rhythm, color, and spatial awareness—in a single, uniquely powerful manner. When we combine it with the vision board exercise, our goals become clearer, more impressed in our unconscious mind, and more memorable as they gain tremendous energy. In this technique, we always start at the center because this gives your brain freedom to spread out in all directions.

While you are doing this, it is important to stimulate both the left and right hemispheres of your brain—the right with words and whole sentences and the left with symbols, designs and colors.

As in the examples, you can use words, colors, symbols, images. The important thing is that they speak to the purpose of your life, of your dreams and evoke your goals. Don't worry if you don't know how to draw. However, it comes out is fine. The idea is not to make a great design but to make a map that includes your goals. On my website—www.luciagiovannini.com—you can download a free guide for making your map.

BETWEEN HAVING DREAMS AND MAKING THEM COME TRUE

> *A vision without work is but a dream. A task without a dream is just drudgery. A vision with a task is the hope for the future of the world.*
>
> —*From a church in Sussex, England, 1730*

Do you know anyone who has many dreams, a thousand goals but has never put any of them into practice? This risk does exist. On one hand, we find people who continually work to satisfy real needs. They pass their entire lives working, making money, spending it, earning it again, being recognized and approved, searching for a companion, leaving them, searching for another. In all this, they are capable, but they are not happy. They have lost the significance of their life.

On the other hand, there are individuals who seem to have great significance, great ideals, but are not capable of putting them into practice. They dream of peace in the world but there is not a part of their world that works, from finances to their sentimental relationships. And yet they have read many books and taken many classes where they were told that they could become whatever they wanted as long as they really wanted it.

It is not true. If dreaming were enough, we would all be Gandhi or Einstein, or movie stars or, at least, rich and famous.

I'm afraid that this misunderstanding comes from the mistaken interpretation of positive thinking which says that "if I think positively, everything will be ok" or what the new age has called laws of attraction: "Want to increase your earnings? All you have to do is dream and money will come to you, so much so that you will receive a big check in the mail." Try seeing if that works, and, please, if it does, let me know. I know it never worked for me! Unfortunately, these beliefs can lead to huge disappointment. The danger of using a dream to avoid everyday life is very strong. The risk is to continue dreaming for your whole life.

What sparked this misconception is the conviction that external reality does not exist but is totally created by our beliefs. In other words, some believe that our thoughts directly create the reality in which we live. That is not true, at least not completely . It is more correct to say that, by the meanings that we give to events, we create our perception, which, in turn, influences the external reality. As we will see in the axes of change, it is basic that dreams lead us to action and to the enrichment of our daily lives, our relationships, our finances and our health.

For this, vision is not enough even if it is an important step. For it to happen, we need to plan, prepare and act, exactly as Andrew did. That which we do and how we do it is just as important as our dream.

THE SEVEN STEPS

> *Energy is the essence of life. Every day you decide how to use it to establish what you want, what you need in order to reach that goal and to maintain your focus.*
>
> —*Oprah Winfrey*

Now that we are aware of the forces of self-realization from our soul and have awakened our dreams and designed our vision, there are seven steps that should be followed to transform all this work into achievable goals. These seven rules come from behavioral and cognitive psychological research, from the Neurolinguistic Programming and Neuro-semantics, and are the results of the most advanced studies that exist at the moment in the field of human resources.

They are the key components that will help you to go beyond your dreams. Thanks to how specific they are, in fact, they will allow you to identify with more clarity that which you want and to actualize a true programming of your physiology and neurology toward your desired goals. At the end of the explanation of each step, you will find questions to apply to your vision.

The first step is to see your objectives positively.

Read these three phrases.

- I am no longer sick.
- I am healed.
- My body is healthy.

What difference do you notice? Which is the strongest, the most definitive, the most effective of the three? And which is the weakest, the most uncertain? What images does it bring to mind?

If your affirmation contains words of healing or healthy, automatically our attention will be drawn to them rather than to the concept of sickness. As we saw in the paragraph dedicated to the importance of establishing clear goals, the mind follows the direction that we give it. It is necessary then to express our goals in positive terms.

In the chapter about the instruments of transformation, we will talk more deeply about the magic of language and we will discover how to use it in a powerful way each and every day.

Question guide:

- Does the description of your goals contain negativity?

The key question to make it positive is:

- What else would you like instead? It may help to ask yourself:
- Where would you like to be?
- Who would you like to be?
- What do you want to become?
- What are you moving toward?

The second step is to make sure that your goals are specific and that they are in sensory terms.

In other words, detail your goals by describing them in such a way that they can be seen, touched or felt. The human brain works principally through the sensory system (images, sounds, and sensations). We have seen that all information arrives to our brain by the five senses.

Too often I have heard people express their goals in such a vague way that they seem invisible. "I want a better life" is not an objective. What exactly do you mean by better? In what sense? What do I see, feel, hear around me when my life is better? Is the description of your goals specific enough and expressed in sensory terms enough to become a film? It should be and you should be able to see it, feel it and perceive it in your mind.

The idea of involving all the senses in the description of your objectives will help you use many more neuron connections. The more of your nervous system that is involved, the more powerful will the programming be toward success.

In the summer of 1999, in a remote village of Bolivia, I had the great opportunity to participate in a series of ceremonies in honor of Mother Earth or *Pachamama*, as she is called by the Indians. These celebrations lasted many days and were held at over four thousand meters' altitude at the top of a sacred mountain that was reachable only by following a very steep and narrow path. My friend and I were the only foreigners and while climbing, or better crawling, up the mountain, we were surrounded by ancient *kallawayas,* the local shamans. The term kallawayas is thought to derive from the ancient Aymara language and means doctor. These elders often travel by foot for miles and miles to heal patients with herbal infusions that they gather from among thousands in the forests. Their medicine must work well because, despite their age, to see them, you would think that the path was flat the way they chatted and laughed happily and went so fast that we almost could not keep up. Even though I was almost thirty years younger than they were, I was exhausted from fatigue and panted while trying to follow them.

Apparently, the knowledge handed down by the kallawayas and their rituals go back to pre-Incan times.

Some of the villages are so isolated and difficult to get to that they escaped Spanish domination. That way, with no external pollution, their ancient culture has been able to keep the purity of its origins. After thinking that I would die over and over, we finally arrived at the top of the mountain. Gradually, the clearing was filled with hundreds of campers with their colored ponchos. They probably came from all over Bolivia because most of them seemed to have travelled for days and days. They all brought their dreams in hope that the Pachamama would be able to make them real.

Before long, the ceremony began. After a general blessing and an invocation to the saints of the region, came the moment of prayers. Every person could make his own request. Some wanted a better harvest, some the healing of a family member, some to meet their soul mate. Can you imagine my surprise when I learned that every request had to be requested wearing a costume that best represented their dream and making it tangible before being blessed with herbs, incense, smoke, alcohol and ritualistic gestures and passed to Mother Earth. The kallawayas asked for a doll from a couple who prayed for the power to have a baby. A farmer put a model house on the altar to represent the house he wished for. Someone who wished for prosperity represented his desire with a pack of fake money and so on. Every objective could be touched, seen and felt with the five senses.

I wonder if the elders already knew the complex mechanisms of the human mind.

Question guide:

- Are you using all your senses while you think of and describe your goal?
- Are you able to transform your map into a film?
- What do you see when you achieve your goals? Who is by your side? Where are you? What details do you see in the film?
- What do you feel physically when you reach your goals? What sensations do you have? What odors, aromas, tastes are there?

- What do you feel emotionally when you achieve your objectives? Where do you feel them in your body? How do they make you feel?
- What sounds, voices do you hear when you arrive at your goals? Are there people talking around you? What are they saying? What are you saying to yourself?

The third step is that the objectives are highly motivating and that they are under your personal control.

The objective must be able to be started and maintained by you and must be about you and not depend on other people. Many get depressed exactly because their goals are unrealistic.

At a course a few years ago, Loredana, a young girl from a town near Torino, Italy, said that her dream was to marry Brad Pitt. Do you think this dream could be transformed into a goal? Apart from the fact that it is very unlikely that it would come true, it would be necessary for Brad Pitt to agree to it. To work toward a similar objective would mean wasting time and interfering in the lives of others. We asked Loredana to understand which of Brad Pitt's characteristics, physical and not, fascinated her and to make a list that could become the basis of a real objective: to start a sentimental relationship with a man who had similar characteristics.

The objective that you decide on must involve you, and, if it includes someone else, the other person must consent.

To give you an idea, here are some examples of objectives, other than marrying Brad Pitt, that cannot be under your control: that our workers or colleagues are always the best (or that our children win the soccer tournament or that they are promoted getting all As); that we always make other people happy (our children, partner, parents, etc.).

Does this surprise you? Do you have similar objectives? Here are some ways for you to transform them: to be the best and give the best of yourself and your experience to your workers or your children; to be a loveable and available person who supports others. In both cases, then, you need to better specify what you mean, how this can happen, what will help you understand that it has happened and so on (see the second step).

Usually, at the end of my objectives, I add a little formula that, up to now, has worked magic and allowed me to clearly define what I want without being too rigid or manipulating of other people: that this or something better will happen for me or the other people involved. The idea is to achieve the greatest good for all. I personally believe that, if the final result is good for all and the benefits go beyond yourself, the system will somehow help you.

If the objective is established and maintained by you, it means that it is within your power zone (remember that seeking and asking for help is within your power zone) and that you are one hundred per cent responsible, so you have no excuse to give it up.

Frank is enrolled in the second year of engineering but is way behind in completing his exams. He feels very guilty because his parents are supporting him but finds it hard to study and uses every excuse to avoid it. "It's strange," he says, "The rest of my life is perfect. It is only with my studies that I cannot get the results I want." When he designed his vision, there was no trace of being an engineer in his future. His map, curiously enough, was full of animals. His dream was to open a shelter for abandoned animals, but his family insisted on a degree. During his next class, Frank decided to start the shelter. By his second session, his degree seemed hidden in a small corner of his map.

Will it be highly motivating for Frank? I'm afraid not. His interests and his heart and passion are elsewhere. "It's clear," says Lisa, who knows Frank's parents, "but if Frank wanted to graduate, and for some reason he could really do it, how could he transform it into a highly motivational objective?"

Usually, I don't like to answer this type of question with their many ifs and buts—and if it does not come from the maker of the map. If it had been Frank who asked it, I would have answered. But I understand that within her question, Lisa has another question that refers to her and is much broader.

How can you make useful objectives (like having a healthier life, doing physical activity and going on a diet as in Lisa's case) highly motivating?

If you want that, we will talk about it more deeply in the section dedicated to motivation, in the axes of change in due time.

Question guide:

- Are your objectives made by yourself?
- Are they within your power zone?
- Can they be started and maintained by you through your thoughts, emotions, words and actions?
- How important is your vision? Is it motivating enough?

The fourth step is to define the milestones, make a plan of action, and act on it.

This step will help you to be sure that your goal is realistic. Too many times people become frustrated because some of their goals are not reachable. "But didn't you tell us that we had to go back to dreaming?" Lisa asks argumentatively. I expected this question from her.

Yes, of course, goals start from dreams, but, while they are becoming objectives, it is important that we make sure that they are realistic. This does not stop us from widening our horizons to new possibilities; actually, it will help us to continue to dream while keeping our feet well planted on the ground. Be careful: the line between the two is very fine.

Marica, a young single mom, made herself the objective of having 100,000 dollars in her bank account in six months. This amount would make her feel sure that she would be able to take care of herself and her child.

"How much do you have in the bank now?" I asked her.

"Fifteen hundred dollars," she answered.

"And how much do you make a month?"

"Twelve hundred dollars."

"How much are you able to save?"

"Nothing."

"Do you have investments?"

"No."

"Nothing else?"

"No."

"Are you thinking of getting another job to earn more money?"

"No, I would not have time."

Is it realistic that Marica would have the money she wanted in the bank in six months? Of course, she could win the lottery, but how probable is that? And is it under her personal control?

Through a plan of action, Marica has been able to realize that her goal has to be modified and divided into many small steps.

Even if the objective is realistic, often the gap between us and the finish line is so great that it seems unachievable. Defining the intermediary steps makes it easier. The higher the objective seems, the more important it is to divide it into small steps.

Even a thousand mile walk begins with a step. Step by step, we can reach the top of any staircase, even the steepest. Have you divided your objective into small enough steps to make it achievable? Or are the single steps still too high for you?

If you want to lose weight, it is useless to decide to not eat for a whole month. It would be very unlikely that you could do it and the result would be that you would feel frustrated because you could not achieve your goal. As a first objective, you could, instead, decide that within three days you would make an appointment with a dietician and that within a week you would start to follow a diet of your choice and that you would go to the gym for one hour three times a week on your lunch break. On Saturday you would go shopping by foot.

This is a method that we know and apply with success in many areas. For example, in our studies and in sports, we are used to setting milestones. No one would expect to be fluent in a new language after only a week of study or to win a ski tournament after only three lessons. If we want to become ski champions, we know that our first goal is the training slope, then the easy slopes and finally the harder ones.

Why not do the same in life? Having a good plan of action has the advantage that every day we know what to do to get closer to our goal. What is your next step?

After that, all you have to do is put into practice that which you have written and decided upon.

Question guide:

- Have you divided your objectives into tiny steps?
- What are the intermediary steps of each of your single goals?
- How big are these steps? Do you think you should divide them even more?
- What is your plan of action?
- What will you do differently tomorrow?

The fifth step is to determine the resources you will need.

What do you need to reach your objectives? What abilities will you need to develop? Who should you become?

I have never been described as a loquacious person. I love to read and be in silence. My perfect day is being in solitude surrounded by nature. As soon as I decided to give courses, it quickly became clear to me that I would have to acquire new resources, one of which was a priority: I would have to learn to talk—and in public no less! It was imperative that I learn to communicate effectively as well, so I started out to learn.

Developing one's own capacities influences our identity. While I was defined as a quiet person earlier, now I know that that was only a part of me and that I can choose how to be depending on the situation. Without relinquishing my nature, now I have more options to choose from. Depending on the occasion, I can go through the day silently, chat with friends or speak to thousands of people. Imagine playing a piano. At the beginning, we are limited to playing only one or two notes. When we expand our capabilities, we have the entire keyboard at our finger tips.

Obviously, this can work in reverse: our capabilities influence what we believe.

For many years I was convinced that I had no lung capacity or resistance. After running seven or eight minutes, my lungs seemed ready to explode. Then, to get ready for hiking the Peruvian mountains, I started to train every day, and, to my great surprise, after a while, I was able to run for almost an hour at a time.

Each time we activate a new capacity, our beliefs of ourselves change and our whole identity is enhanced.

Now I don't say that I have no stamina. Probably, I will never participate in the New York marathon but jogging has become one of my favorite pastimes, and, above all, I know that, if I have improved my running, I can get better in other areas as well. It's not a question of age or of capacity. We have many of those potential neuron connections at our disposition, and we don't need a hundred lives to use them all.

Make a list of all the resources that you will need to realize your dream and remember all the times that you were able to activate them.

Every one of us has a huge toolbox with all the necessary tools needed for change, some are right in plain sight and ready to use. Others are at the bottom of the box, dusty and covered with rust, but it's up to us to get moving and find them and bring them back to life. If we can do it once, we will know that we can do it again.

If you can't remember times when you have activated resources like that, then look around you to find people who have. Find one or two role models, men or women who have reached your goal and have been an inspiration to you. Learn from them. Examine and then imitate their strategies. Find out how they did it. What is their life like? How do they use their time? What are their beliefs, moods, words, actions?

If you don't know anyone at all like this, then activate your imagination. What type of person could achieve your goal? What characteristics would they need to possess?

Question guide:

- What resources do you need?
- How can you develop them?
- Who do you have to become?
- Do you know anyone that had achieved these goals?
- What resource and/or capacities did they use?

What other resources may be helpful?

- Have you ever done anything similar?
- Who do you think could help you?
- What will you do differently?

The sixth step is to take stock and discover a secondary advantage

Is your vision balanced? Does it bring improvement to all areas of your life, or are there parts that will suffer?

Whatever transformation, even the smallest, implies a change in the existing balance, something that many people try to avoid at all costs.

Even failure has its paradoxical advantages: it gives us the right to complain, to get attention and help from others; we can avoid the discomfort of joining and protect ourselves from the risks of change.

As we have seen in earlier changes, often there are old parts of us that are still screaming their needs, so we end up having conflicting goals. We feel as though we are divided within, as if we are a horse-drawn carriage going in opposite directions. It is not at all pleasant.

It is important to be aware of these issues and address them. In general, the rule would be to find different ways to satisfy the real needs and leave the old and dysfunctional ones behind. If we don't do that, they will always be a part of us and will continue to sabotage our objectives.

* * *

Recently in Bless You International, our objective was to increase the number of courses we were giving, especially abroad since we love to travel and relate to diverse cultures. When we reviewed this objective, we realized that there was a secondary advantage of leaving things as they were. We could stay at home more and have more free time. We realized that, although we wanted to amplify our activities, this was an advantage that we wanted to keep.

We had to find new solutions. We thought about having most of our classes open to the public and close to home, so we could avoid travel time and counterbalance the time that we were travelling around the world. We now realize that, when making our choices, we must consider even free time; otherwise, we risk unconsciously sabotaging our work. With this clearly in mind, now we feel assured in opening new markets abroad and with all our possible new projects.

Think carefully about how your current status (not what you desire but the problem you are now experiencing) satisfies your needs. Be honest with yourself—because if you had been honest with yourself earlier, the change would have already happened.

This may sound strange but it happens all the time. For example, someone who wants to lose weight may believe that heavy people are nicer, always the most pleasant or they may use their weight as a defense against intimacy.

Someone who wants to quit smoking may discover that, thanks to the cigarettes, he is less anxious or he feels less alone. And so it goes…

Question guide:

- What effect will reach your goals have on other parts of your life?
- What will you gain and what will you lose? What are you afraid of losing by reaching your goals?
- Are the goals you have in harmony with your values, your health and your well-being?
- Are your objectives in line with the kind of person you want to be, with the purpose of your life?

Discover the Repercussions of Your Goals

For each of your objectives, take a clean page in your diary and answer the following questions:

- What risks do you face by achieving___ (my objective)? What consequences will it bring me, my relationships, my work, my family/ society/the world?
- Am I ready to face that?
- What other resources do I need? (See the paragraph about stabilizing and activating resources.)
- What advantage is there to keeping the status quo?
- Do you want to keep this advantage?
- (If you answered "yes") In what other ways can I keep it?
- (If you answered "no") In what way can I let it go more easily?
- What resources do I need to do it?
  How can I activate them?

It is necessary to answer honestly.
Once you have answered, react accordingly.

The seventh step is to establish a tracking procedure.

How will you know when you have achieved your goal? It may seem paradoxical, and yet, in the busyness of everyday life, we risk reaching our goal without even realizing it. The risk is to live life dissatisfied, waiting for something to happen and not realizing that something is already happening.

Question guide:

- What are the specific parameters that will let you know when you have reached your goal?
- When will you say that you are satisfied in respect to your vision?
- What will tell you that you have arrived at the finish line?

A BRIDGE TO THE FUTURE

> *You have your paints and you have your brushes;*
> *draw paradise and go inside.*
>
> —*Nikos Kazantzakis*

Now that we have transformed our dreams into objectives and have developed our strategies to reach them, all that's left is to create a plan to make it actually happen and get to work.

As airplane pilots use a flight simulator to learn how to fly, every human being has a kind of simulator of life—the imagination. It allows us to live out specific experiences and to train ourselves to face them best.

Cognitive sciences have long studied the effect of imaginative therapy and applied creative visualization in various situations with great results. One of these studies was done in the United States with three basketball teams. For a whole season, the first team practiced as usual. The second practiced only half of their usual time and, during the other half, used imaginative therapy. While comfortable sitting on an easy chair, the athletes were asked to imagine every detail of being at the game, to score points and to play like champions. The third team completely substituted physical training with imaginative training only. Rather than doing physical exercise and practicing baskets, they worked on strategy. During the day, the athletes trained by visualizing playing the game the best they could.

A confirmation of the effect of imagination therapy was quick to arrive.

The second team, the one that had used both physical training and imaginative, had the best results for the whole season. The other two were tied even though the third never once trained on the court.

On the tails of these studies, in 1980, the Russian Olympic team discovered that the athletes who won the most medals were those who regularly practiced visualization. It seems that when we practice the exercise of visualization, we have less probability for error, as if the mind's eye was capable of demonstrating the right actions, and, in this way, the brain became informed as to how to guide the body in reality. This is what Daniel Goleman wrote in his book *Social Intelligence:* "When we go over an action mentally—like practicing a speech that we have to give or imagining our best golf shots—the same neurons in the brain's cortex come into play as the ones that would be activated if the speech were really being given or if the hole-in-one were really made. To simulate an action in the brain is equivalent to actually doing it."

* * *

Even though most of these experiments have been done in the world of sports, the application of imaginative therapy is much broader.

The principal of this simple technique is based on the fact that, in our unconscious mind, there is no difference between something actually experienced and something vividly imagined. In both cases, new synapses are created. If, to this, we add high emotional involvement, the process becomes even more powerful.

In our case, to create the desired results, we will make both a plan of action and do imaginative therapy, like the second basketball team in the experiment.

CROSS THE BRIDGE, AND DO IT AS OFTEN AS YOU CAN!

Imagination and faith are the same thing. They give life to our hopes and make the invisible reality.

—*John V. Taylor*

Once you have completed your map, put it in a place where you will see it as often as possible. And when you cannot physically see it, imagine it in your mind. The idea is to imagine the particulars of your objectives as if they were already achieved and to feel the resulting sensations and emotions. Every time you do that, your bridge becomes stronger and stronger and easier to follow.

Are you afraid that you cannot visualize? Every human being can do it. It's primarily about remembering and bringing to life your thoughts.

If I ask you to remember your kitchen or your living room right now, would you be able to do it? Maybe some of you would evoke the images, the forms and the colors more easily, while others find it easier to remember the sounds or the feelings. That's enough to do this exercise. You do not have to do anything more than bring to life your dreams and the realization of your objectives.

One thing that will help is to relax. Body and mind live most closely when we are relaxed; when one relaxes, the other benefits as well.

Crossing the bridge to the future becomes easier if our entire system is relaxed. To do that, you don't need much time. I don't expect you to spend whole days visualizing. It's more important to have brief visualizations, even two or three minutes at a time, and repeat them often throughout the day.

Take advantage of the human ability to create habits and insert your visualizations into your daily life. You can, for example, take your map to your bedroom and do the exercises before you get up in the morning and then again before you go to sleep at night. Or you can stick it on your bathroom mirror and look at it while brushing your teeth, putting on your make-up or shaving. Or you can put it in your wallet and imagine your objectives while going to work or waiting in line at the grocery store.

As you can see, you can't use the classic excuse "I don't have time."

Find solutions that work for you. Invent them. Personalize them. Be creative. For example, Nicoletta, one of our trainers, took a picture of her map and uses it as her screensaver on her computer and her cell phone. Emanuel, a dear friend and founder of an association with which we collaborate, made a copy of his map, reduced it in size and laminated it. Now it has the shape of a credit card and he brings it with him everywhere.

"Why is it important to be able to see it so often? Isn't it enough to have made it?" I still can't understand if Lisa is doubtful or if she is behaving like a lazy child who is trying to get away from doing homework. For sure, she is very combative; on one hand, she wants to change, but, on the other, she is afraid. She's gives the impression that she is always driving with the hand brake engaged. Of course, it is important to have deeply reflected on your dreams and to have put them down on paper. To stay in contact with our vision helps us to stay on course even more. This is simply not a magical process; it is not about blowing fairy dust on our dreams. From the psychological point of view, this exercise will help to confirm your intentions, to mobilize your energies, conscious and unconscious, and to focus toward your objectives.

Do it and you will see for yourself the difference in your life.

CHAPTER 6

THE AXES OF CHANGE

I will show you the path toward liberation.
Know that liberation depends on yourself.

—Buddha

At this point, in all probability, beyond establishing your vision, you have also identified the reasons why—and the new behaviors needed—to achieve change.

Now, it's time to transform your thoughts into action.

But, why is it so difficult to change—even if we have understood (better late than never!) that certain ways of thinking and behaving are damaging our well-being?

Why—even if we know we should exercise—is it so difficult to put down the remote, get up from the couch, put on our running shoes and go running?

Why—when we own a closet full of shoes that we won't be able to wear in the next ten lives—do we continue to spend our money on more?

Why—even if everybody knows that potato chips are bad for you—do we continue to eat lots of them and abandon every new diet within a month?

Why is it so difficult to change old habits?

ESCAPE FROM DEPENDENCE

Nora Volkow, director of the American National Institute on Drug Abuse, has dedicated her life to research dependence and, in particular, has spent the last fifteen years studying what it is that makes it so difficult to change habits. She did not look for the solution in external factors or circumstances but concentrated her inquiries on the human brain. And there she found the answer: dopamine.

Dopamine is a neurotransmitter, a chemical product of the brain that transmits information from one cell to another. Its job is to teach the brain what we want (cigarette? potato chips? instant pleasure?) and push us toward getting it. Obviously, dopamine cannot ask itself if that behavior is good for us or not.

All this happens in two phases. When we experience something pleasurable (like eating potato chips or any other pleasurable action), dopamine is produced, some of which goes through our neurons until it reaches the brain's memory center. There, a connection is created between that action and the pleasure. Researchers would say that that action (in our example, the eating of potato chips) has become "salient". At that point, every time we come across them, even if our brain says, "they are not good for me; I should not eat them", our brain registers "dopamine!"

Here's where the second phase kicks in: the dopamine controls the part of the brain responsible for desire, motivation and decision making. Once the potato chips have become salient, every time we see or smell them, our brain registers an increase in dopamine which pushes us toward continuing to eat them. As soon as we do eat them, our brain produces more dopamine which reinforces the memory that made them salient the first time. And the cycle of dependence continues to feed itself. We end up having an increase in dopamine which will push us to look for potato chips even when we see a McDonald's sign.

"Dopamine is the chemical substance of motivation," states Nora Volkow, "and this mechanism is perfectly logical. If we had to create a species and insure that it survived, that it is nourished and that it reproduces itself, how could we do it if not by a system based completely on pleasure pushing us toward the repetition of those actions? Dopamine makes sure that these behaviors become automatic and, so, the species lasts. It is genius!"[12] The problem is that the same mechanism is valid for every behavior and in almost every area of life that gives us instant gratification. It's like we have seen; even every dysfunctional behavior has its way of bringing pleasure, rewarding us. This is why it is so difficult to change beliefs and habits. To do it you must go against one of the basic neurological mechanisms. To not do it, however, means letting the brain's chemicals guide our life.

As usual, the choice is in our hands.

"Andrew was so angry that I had signed him up for the course, and, to be honest, I was skeptical, too. The idea to have long-lasting results simply meant having a clear vision and some affirmation of things that I'd read in books seemed much too simplistic. Then I saw how he changed and I was shocked. I realized that my information was not enough, that there was more," Lisa finally opened up and began to understand.

---

[12] From the article "Why is it so damn hard to change?" by Rebecca Skloot, in *The Oprah Magazine*, January 2007.

I understand. It is true that the naive and superficial belief that we can get results with only a minimum of effort risks creating misunderstandings and can end up blocking real change. If the habits and dysfunctional beliefs have been with us for many years and are continually fed by the dopamine cycle, it takes will, perseverance, commitment and knowledge to replace them with new ways. The way to realize our dreams is not at all simple and direct; it often resembles the course of a river that goes toward the ocean. It is tortuous and discontinuous.

CAN WE PUT CHANGE IN OUR SUITCASE?

We talk of making change, but are we capable of embracing it and taking change with us? Or stocking up on it at the supermarket? Or borrowing it?

Even though we speak of it as if it were a thing, in reality, change is an interactive process that is very complex. It involves many different variables, takes place on many levels and involves the great risk of relapse.

How many times have you sworn to yourself that you would change and maybe did for a short period, but then, seduced by dopamine, you found yourself exactly where you were in the beginning?

To avert this risk and better confront the journey toward transformation, we need a prototype which will indicate as precisely as possible how change works, what the variants are, what the mechanisms involved are and what the activities and phases to cross are. We must understand how to trick the brain's chemistry and make the basic mechanisms of neurology work to our advantage.

In this chapter, you will find a model that will dissect the structure of change and its cornerstones. This work is based on the most recent research of cognitive psychology and, in particular, Neuro-Semantics and Meta-Coaching of Michael Hall and Michelle Duval.[13]

This model has served as a path for thousands of people to successfully navigate the labyrinth of change.

Whatever change we want to make, we must go through precise phases. You have already had an opportunity to deepen your understanding of some in the preceding pages. Now you will discover others and see how the various components interact. In this way, you will be able to see just where you are right now and put it into a larger context. You will then be able to evaluate on your own which phase you are in and how you must navigate within the axes of change.

When one axis is very strong, sometimes it's all you need to start change. For example, a tumor on the lungs may be enough to push you to completely stop smoking. But, usually multiple factors are required to push us to change. Think about the changes that you have made in your life. How did they happen? What was the stimulus? What phase did you start in? Did you think about it? Did you have a precise strategy from the outset or did you act impulsively and then saw what happened? Did you go toward what you desired or did you run from something that you did not want? Were you sustained by the motivation through to the end or did it dwindle after a while? Can you easily consolidate your results?

Most of the time it is necessary that all the elements, which we will discover in the following pages, work together until the transformation is solid and permanent. In some cases, you will discover that is it possible to reverse the order of these factors and the results won't change. We can, in fact, enter the circuit of change by any of the axes, and, often, we must use them at the same time.

---

[13]   *Meta-Coaching: The Axes of Change.*

To be clear, though, I have preferred to explore them one at a time in their natural order—the one that occurs most commonly.

AWARENESS

> *If something external hurts you, it is not the thing that disturbs you but it is what you think about it.*
>
> *—Marc Aurelius*

On a superficial level, it's relatively easy to exercise awareness, especially if it's regarding potato chips; we can't avoid realizing that we are eating them. It's more complex to go deeper though and understand why we continue to eat them and what meaning we have connected to them. Then, if we talk about thought patterns and beliefs about ourselves and the world, we enter a realm of awareness that is much more complicated. Our behaviors and their consequences are not always so obvious.

"Everybody tells me to go out and meet people; friends try to set up dates for me but it's useless. No man will ever fall in love with me. Just like I'll never get the promotion I want. I don't even want to think about it; I'll just be disappointed. Why am I so unlucky?" Sarah looks at us while running her hands through her long blond hair with long—held tears falling from her blue eyes. She looks like a porcelain statue, maybe because of the immaculate color of her skin. Fashion magazines would definitely define her as overweight and, watching her eat, it's not difficult to imagine how food has become her outlet and her main gratification. You get the sensation that, by way of eating, she's trying to get all the nutrition that life is not giving her.

She is single, about forty and her greatest desire is to find a companion and start a family. Her sister Carmen is an established stylist, has been happily married for ten years, but, even before marrying, she never lacked suitors. She was always considered the most beautiful of the town and Sarah felt like the chubby, ugly and unlucky sister. She brought this label with her even when she came to our course. Every day something happened that, according to her, proved it.

"Recently," she tells us, "I went out with Josh, the new director of the bank near where I work. I counted on the fact that, being new to town, he would not know anything about me or my sister, but even our first date was a disaster."

She explains that during dinner, Josh received a few phone calls from work, some of which lasted, according to her, too long. Sarah started to think that if, instead of herself, the beautiful and intelligent Carmen had been there, he would not have been on the phone so much and would have been careful to dedicate all his attention to her and not waste even a minute of their time together. These thoughts gave way to a mood of resentment that translated into cold and sarcastic comments for the rest of the evening. "I was angry and very offended," she commented. "How could I not be?" It's useless to say that Josh never asked her out again. "Men are all the same. Even he realized how ugly I am," was her bitter comment.

As we have seen in previous chapters, most of the functioning of our psyche occurs in the unconscious without our awareness. If we do not realize that we need to change and if we are not aware of our thought patterns and what limits us, change will never happen.

Awareness is decidedly the foundation of change, and this is why so much of this book is dedicated to it.

"Well, I have a companion, my health, beautiful children and no financial problems. Yet I am always depressed.

Things were not going well with Andrew and the children were hard to take care of. At least that's how I saw it, what I told myself," Lisa confided. She and Sarah were chosen to do certain exercises together and seemed to get along. "In the last course, I realized that I was wearing distorted glasses and that a part of my life was being guided by old conditionings, the part of toxic Matrix that told me that I was not a good mother, that Andrew was not a good companion and so on. I decided to discover who I really was. At home, I wrote down all my emotions and what caused them in my diary. There were only a couple of times when things really went badly, but no more. I realized that I had spread those couple of times to my whole life. I took another look at my notes and remembered what we had talked about. I was not sure if it was pervasiveness or permanence, or maybe both. Then I started to laugh. What difference does the exact definition make? And once I realized that, a light went off. Then I began to note all the occasions that make me feel well, in which I smiled and was calm. There were many. Focusing my attention consciously on them, I found many more."

It is with awareness that we can separate the experience of what happens (like Josh who got many phone calls during dinner) from the interpretations and meanings that we give them (he was on the phone because I'm ugly, he's poorly behaved, if it were my sister Carmen instead, he would not do it) and from the reactions that we have (dry comments, impatient tone of voice).

In some cases, this is all that is needed to make a big change. To bring forward the dysfunctional parts of matrix, individualize the damaging beliefs, understand the arbitrary meanings and toxic interpretations that we have attributed to something or someone, and we are brought to change.

In the end, actions and moods stem from thoughts, and, since we are thinkers, we can change things as soon as we become aware of them. The mere fact of being aware of our moods changes them; passion becomes compassion, anger become decision, fear becomes action and confusion takes on a life of clarity and so on.

It's not rare then that these moments of intense awareness lead to some real awakenings. These are the moments in which we have a realization, in which we spontaneously realize that something has always been there, right under our nose, but our blinders had prohibited us from seeing it. Gestalt calls it "Aha! Moments," the best definition I can imagine.

FOR WHOM THE BELL TOLLS?

What brings us to that moment, and, vice versa, what blocks our understanding of it?

Awareness comes from our mind's capacity to observe and reflect, to come out of the situation that we are in for a moment and take stock of where we are.

When we direct this observation internally, we enter the function of auto reflection—the exploration of our thoughts, actions and moods. But often we are so busy that our attention is continually elsewhere.

The Vietnamese monk Thich Nhat Hanh gave life to a movement called Mindfulness Bell, which is an invitation to awareness. In his French monastery, Plum Village, twice a day at a determined time, a bell rings. At this sound, whoever is at the monastery has the task of interrupting whatever they are doing and taking a few deep breaths. This way, people are induced to bring their attention to the present and to think of their own actions and their own thoughts.

The whole part of this book dedicated to the frames of the mind is a bell of mindfulness just like writing every day in your diary and answering the questions that you find at the end of the exercises.

Acceptance and awareness are closely linked. To truly accept something, you must first be aware of it. Exactly as it is for acceptance, until we are aware, it is fundamental that all judgment is avoided. To judge our behaviors and our beliefs inhibits our understanding and makes us defensive which inhibits access to the matrix. True awareness comes from trying to understand and accepting reality for what it is, not for how we wish it to be.

Stefano was considered a promising tennis star by all. Not more than an adolescent and very prepared physically, he had practiced sports since he was a child, but, as soon as he started to take the sport seriously, his performance in tournaments declined drastically and this was a problem. For a while, the boy had been in a downward spiral; his results got worse, and, because of this, so did his mood. After refusing many times, his coach convinced him to take coaching lessons.

In our first sessions, we asked the boy to observe how his thoughts and mood changed in various moments of the game, but this exploration seemed too difficult for him. As soon as he was aware of his reactions, Stefano became trapped in a web of judgment and became even more nervous. Only when he started to observe himself without judging, without the weight of expectations, but with the curiosity of a simple spectator, could he live the "Aha! moment." In that moment, it was clear to him that the key to change, for him, was to abandon the fear of judgment by others.

Besides allowing us to know ourselves better and to make clear where we are, another important role of awareness is to indicate what we need to change and where we need to focus. As we experienced when we were making the map of our vision, this allows us to organize our attention and give purpose and direction to our actions.

For many years, traditional psychology was completely centered on awareness because it was thought to be an essential element for healing. The whole school of Freud and that of psychoanalysis were focused on the study of causes, on understanding what was not working and on the reasons that we behaved in a certain way. Only lately have we discovered that all of that, even if important, is often not sufficient enough to change things.

In this case, the problem is not in ignoring the cause or in not knowing what to do, but it is in not doing what you do know. In other words, sometimes we are very aware that we behave in a dysfunctional way, even knowing the origins of our actions and our thought patterns, but we're still not able to change. Does it sound familiar?

Often, knowledge by itself is not enough to sustain us during the whole process of change.

Knowledge has an extremely important role during the process of change but often it is only the beginning, not the end. This is why it is important that other phases are also used.

MOTIVATION

> *One can choose to go back toward safety or to go ahead toward growth; growth must be chosen continually and fear must be won continually.*
>
> —*Abraham Maslow*

Recently I realized that I cannot expect that others will change; it must be me who does it first. If I see myself as unattractive, unlucky and incapable, this is what others will see in me as well. If I continue this way, the situation will only get worse." I cannot believe that these words are coming from Sarah. And it has not even been a month since the first course!

We know how motivation works from the physiological point of view—by the production of dopamine. If it's true that this process guides us in our life choices, it is also true that once we know the mechanisms, we can guide them using them to our advantage. Motivation is no more than the emotion that is behind every kind of change, and, because of this, plays a fundamental role. It is the energy motive that gets us out of our comfort zone. Without energy to help us, dreams don't get very far. In the end, it's only when we feel that we must move (emotion derives from the Latin *emovere* which means "to move") that we change. Logic makes us reason but emotions make us act.

Its development is innate: we tend to distance ourselves from anything that gives us pain and go toward things that give us pleasure. We change because we want something, we desire new experiences, we are inspired by our dreams, we are captured by a vision or we begin to believe in it and invest time and energy.

Or, like Sarah, we change when we have suffered enough, we can't take any more, we are obligated, we have no other choice or no other exits.

Which of these cases sounds like you? Are you part of the club that is pushed by the whip or the one that goes toward the carrot?

Silvia, a friend of mine, has said she wants to quit smoking for years. She's tried various techniques, always without success. "There's no hope," she said to me the other day, "with me it does not work." So I asked her if an incentive of a hundred dollars a month would help.

"A hundred dollars a month?" Silvia answered. "It still would not work. Unfortunately, I'm not determined, perseverant. It's not in my nature."

"How about a thousand dollars a month?" I said. "A thousand dollars? I'm not sure but I can try." "Ten thousand dollars a month?" I pressed.

"Are you kidding? Of course, I would do it. For ten thousand dollars a month, I would quit immediately."

The problem is not the method or her character; it is the fact that quitting smoking is not a motivating enough objective for Silvia. Ten thousand dollars a month is.

Silvia is careful not to seriously consider the damages caused by smoking. Probably spending some time in a hospital with lung cancer patients would have had the same effect as the ten thousand dollars a month. It would push her to act, to do something.

TENSION AS FUEL?

The axis of motivation is a dance between the drive toward what we want and an escape from what we don't want. As soon as we establish an objective, we also decide that the present state is different from what we desire and the space between the two states becomes evident. This space is usually perceived as a vacuum and often becomes a source of tension.

How would you live with this vacuum? When you think of your objectives, do you feel tension, anxiety, stress, worry? If you feel tension, don't worry; it's natural. Be aware though that there are only two ways to manage this feeling.

The first is used by many who confuse this vacuum with a negative emotion and consequently cannot handle it. So they try to eliminate it, but the only way to do that is to lessen their vision, give up their objectives and stop believing in their dreams. In this way, the tension will diminish but so will the n/um, the vital energy, and, in a short time, it will be replaced by inertia, procrastination, and lack of initiative. When these symptoms are present, it means that either we are too focused on the problems and we don't allow ourselves to dream, or we cannot tolerate the tension that the dance of motivation entails.

The second way to handle this sensation is to learn to live with it, accept it and use the tension as fuel for action. After all, the purpose for change is not simply comfort but moreover to expand one's possibilities. To do this, it is fundamental that you are inspired by your vision and make it more effective. The vision, as we have said, includes the objectives but, at the same time, transcends them. It has much broader energy because it includes more solutions than we could imagine and is powered by the purpose of our lives.

When we remain focused on our goal and we accept this feeling of tension, this same tension becomes a source of creative energy.

In this way, the work on our vision becomes fundamental. Are you asking if you have done it correctly? There is an unmistakable sign that will tell you: joy.

A vision is such if it inspires a sense of openness, passion and joy, and, if we allow it, will stay will us from morning to night—all day long.

Does your vision have these characteristics?

If you are still not completely satisfied, continue to think and rethink what you really love, what you like, what gives you joy and amplifies your design with these new elements. And remember to not confuse joy with pleasure; the first is much deeper and longer lasting than the second. At the end of this section, you will find questions that will allow you to review your map more deeply.

Be careful though…remember that an effective vision together with joy brings with it the necessary tension toward its goal. Are you ready to accept it?

We act either because we are attracted by the joy of the vision or because we are prodded by the intolerance of pain.

In fact, sometimes, as in the case of Sarah, we need a strong anti-vision that prods us to say "*enough is enough.*" As we have seen at the beginning of this book, any crisis—be it sentimental, work related or physical—can serve this purpose.

Have you asked yourself how you will end up if you do not change? Dancing on this end of the axis of motivation implies having the courage to look in the face of the harsh reality.

"I can't take it anymore; I'm seriously thinking of separating," Monica confides shortly before the course begins. "The worst thing is that Carlo is convinced that it won't help. He keeps thinking that there's no problem and that things are going well. We've been married for three years, we haven't been intimate for a while and we don't talk without fighting. Our only conversations are about Alex's kindergarten. We have no hobbies in common; we each have our own life. Is this a relationship that is going well? How can he not see it?"

Often, as happened to Carlo, we don't have the energy to confront reality and we prefer not to see what hurts us. When we don't elaborate on the feedback that we receive, we become superficially hyper optimistic, we don't stop to reflect and we risk negating that part of our life. Repression of our emotions starts the refusal of thinking about certain parts of our life. It's a dangerous behavior because not only does it cause us to be unrealistic but also prevents us from completely using the axis of motivation, depriving us of the energy required to activate a transformation.

In case you tend to behave like Carlo and hide your head in the sand, you'll find some questions here that will guide you to take a real inventory of what bothers you and then you can use that as a push toward action.

Motivation Questions

Toward the achievement of the vision

- What happens inside you when you look at the map that you have designed? Does it make you happy? Do you feel a kind of tension?
- Is there something that you would like to achieve? Does your vision include the purpose of your life?
- What ideas inspire and excite you most?
- What most catches your interest?
- If you had one secret passion, what would it be?
- Where would you like to be on your birthday five years from now? In ten years?
- What would you have to do to be able to say that you have lived fully and have had a life full of meaning?
- If a miracle happened tonight, how would you live tomorrow? What would be different?

Away from what we don't want: the inventory of brainteasers

- What parts of your life are not the way you would like them?
- What are you pretending to not know?
- What are you still tolerating that is causing you problems?
- What have you had enough of?
- What excuses are you still using to avoid following your dreams?
- What old strategies and behavior schemes are you still using without getting results?
- How much longer do you want to continue like this?
- What will happen if things don't change?
- Do you want to be in these same conditions thirty years from now?

Quick self-motivation kit in four questions

If you want to increase motivation regarding an action to take or a specific objective:

- What will happen if I do it?
- What won't happen if I don't do it?
- What will happen if I don't do it?
- What won't happen if I do it?

DECISION

> *Not everything that we confront can be changed,*
> *but nothing can change if we don't confront it.*
>
> —*James Baldwin*

"Ever since I was little, I've felt ugly and not good enough, and I ended up believing it, but this way of thinking is useless and only brings disappointment and pain; I've really had enough. I've decided! It's time to change. And I don't want to wait until tomorrow. The time to change is now!" affirmed Sarah while her chubby hands gestured as if they were underlining her words. For the first time, her fragility disappeared and made way for determination.

From zero to ten, how determined are you to change?

The decision comes when we make a commitment to ourselves. That moment is the very center of the transformation. And, with a decision, we say no to the old and yes to the new, giving ourselves permission to change. In general, all this happens after understanding, through reflection, that we are worth something better and that other possibilities exist. Reflection is part of the axis of decision, the careful evaluation of the pros and cons, but also of the resolution and determination without which we will remain blocked in the world of hypothesis.

Has it ever happened to you that you can't change even if you're motivated to do it and perfectly aware of your dysfunctional patterns? Many times, even if the change attracts us, we hesitate—asking ourselves whether or not to proceed, whether or not we have the resources and the necessary time or how much it will cost—and we end up stuck in this hesitancy. If we don't make a clear choice, we open the space to ambivalence and to every type of excuse and loophole.

To take a decision is equal to taking a new direction. This upsets the old stability that kept things in their place and often means renouncing certain secondary benefits (power, privilege, prestige, etc.) as we have seen in the seven steps of the vision.

If we neglect reflection prior to the decision, we'll find ourselves acting impulsively to events without thinking.

And we won't always be happy with the consequences. On the other hand, if we remain blocked in this phase, we won't stop weighing, evaluating, thinking, analyzing and reflecting—without ever being ready for action. The more time passes, the more we are paralyzed and the more we risk giving up on the change. If you find yourself in this situation, don't be alarmed; it just means that you need to take a step backward, back into the axis of motivation, to renew the energy that fuels your decision.

When we implement the decision phase in a balanced manner, every evaluation is designed to generate the most decision-making power and to prepare us for action. Although motivation's fuel is the emotions, when we are in the axis of decision, it is helpful to remember that they are an expression of our self and of our way of thinking in any given moment. As we will see better in the instruments of transformation, emotions are only part of us. Just because we are angry, frustrated or afraid, does not mean that we are that anger, that frustration or that fear. The risk, if we're not careful, is to take decisions that don't really represent us. We are not slaves of our emotions so we can choose whether to act or not.

In the questions area, you will be guided by a model that is very useful for reflection: SWOT where S stands for strengths, W for weaknesses, O for opportunities and T for threats. It is often used in the corporate world, but, in reality, it's very useful even for our interior world and for personal objectives.

The purpose of a SWOT analysis is to provide a method that will guide you through the phase of decision.

THE QUESTIONS OF THE DECISION

Write your answers in a page of your diary. Repeat the same questions for every objective of your vision.

- What are your strengths?
- What do you think of your strengths? How do they make you feel?
- What are your weaknesses? What are your challenges?
- What do you think of your weaknesses? How do they make you feel?
- What are your opportunities? What will happen if you get what you want? What is at stake? What are the pros? What do you want to have happen?
- Why is this important to you? Why do you have this objective? What does it represent for you?
- What are the threats? What are the challenges? What are you afraid might happen? What is the probability that it will happen? And if it happens, what will fol-

low? What is the worst that could happen? What is the most important thing in all of this?

• What will you lose if you don't change, if you don't reach your objective? What will happen if you choose to not change?

CREATION

An action is a thought that comes to life.

—*Paulo Coelho*

"The parts of myself that I like?" Sarah asks. By now, we are in our third course, and, during the last few months, many things have happened in Sarah's life. "Earlier I would have said that there are not any, but, now that I think more about it, I love my eyes, my breasts, my hair, my hands, my sense of humor, my love for humanity, my sweet personality and availability, my ability to listen to people, my generosity and my accurate and detail oriented work. And I am proud because they are not common qualities. At work, I am the oldest and have years of experience. I love my work and I have all the necessary qualities for a promotion. Of course, for this new job I will need to learn French, but I know I can do it."

At every meeting, Sarah tells us about some new positive aspect that she has found in herself. Miraculously, others seem to become aware as well. Her colleagues ask her what has happened. Men don't avoid her anymore; her calendar is actually filling with invitations. Something is changing.

After you understand what to improve and have generated the energy to do it to the point of making a decision, you need a specific plan to bring about the change. It is a step that must come from within us, in our way of thinking that is then to be brought out by our behaviors. It's a change from inspiration to experimentation.

This phase is divided into two parts: the inner creation and the outer creation.

While the first means planning, brainstorming, thinking of options, possibilities and strategies, the second part is pure action.

THE INNER CREATION: THOUGHT

During the process of change, when we continue to face difficulty and resistance in the external world, the first thing to do is to strengthen the internal part of our creation—we must update our system of beliefs by giving it new frames and new meaning to events.

In the earlier phases, did you identify the dysfunctional beliefs and behaviors that you wanted to change? Are you motivated? Have you decided to do it? Now let's create that transformation.

A belief is formed when at least two levels of thought exist. In Sarah's case, in the first level, we find thoughts like: I'm ugly, men don't want me, everything happens to me, I'm not good enough. Added to these are various levels of confirmation: "It's really like this, I'm sure. The fact that Josh was on the phone for so long and that I still haven't gotten a promotion, even after five years, proves it." In every occasion, in other words, we confirm our theory.

To create a transformation, we must first remove the beliefs that are blocking us and unlearn what we have learned, validated and added to our Matrix. The best way to do this is to show ourselves that this information is not accurate. But how?

The first step is to become aware that our beliefs are just that—only ideas—and, as such, can be wrong. Then we must look around for evidence to confirm that this way of thinking is wrong. It's exactly the opposite of what we usually do, when we look around for reasons to confirm our old way of thinking. By discovering evidence to demonstrate how inaccurate our beliefs are, we have the possibility to grow, to generate new alternatives and to find new solutions. This is how inner creation happens.

Often, by changing only one frame, we are able to start a whole revolution in our lives.

THE EXTERNAL CREATION: ACTION!

Whether this is our case or not, we must begin to translate these new beliefs into concrete actions and behave in a way that reflects that which we want to become. What is our next step?

If our plan foresees action, this is the moment to start. And don't fall into the trap of waiting for the right moment to start because it will never be right! Often the problem for many people isn't that we don't know what to do, but it's not doing what we do know. Only by taking action can things change. And it's not important how big a problem or how complicated a situation seems. Often it just takes one action, even a small one, to make the confusion disappear and the solution appear closer.

"Talking does not cook the rice," advises an antique Chinese proverb.

In some new age and pseudo spiritual schools, action is seen as something negative, and between action and contemplation, it seems that the second has more worth. It's as if action were reserved for miserable mortals while the truly evolved don't need action; for them, thought is enough.

I have frequented some people of these groups and heard talk of many grand objectives, of what would be accomplished, of how, through their courses, humanity would be changed. I then met them again years later and nothing had changed—not in their personal lives (their problems were still the same as before and even worse), not in their courses, not in the people who had participated. What happened?

They spent hours talking, visualizing, chanting mantras, making vows, praying, dancing and going into trances. All of these are surely important on their own, but no one had worried about then taking action. Action is fundamental if we want creation to happen. Otherwise, it's the same as buying all the ingredients to make a cake, to prepare the ingredients carefully, mixing them, heating the oven and then . . . never baking the cake.

Many of our courses use, in some way, Neurolinguistic Programming. In NLP, action is so important that one of its reference points is "as if ." The rule is: behave as if. It is impossible to behave for long in a certain way and not become that way. Day by day, that action will permeate your identity. Do you want to become a writer? start writing! Do you want to become a runner? start running! Do you want to be happy? What would you do if you were? Ok, do it!

Of course if we were to bring this to an extreme, there would be a risk. In fact there's no need to say that even the NLP, in some cases, has created low level salesmen devoid of ethics whose only reason for action is the result and for whom the end justifies the means. Need an example? Do you want to be rich? Behave "as if ," and start spending all the money you have. Want to become a trainer? Behave "as if, " and start giving classes; it does not matter if you're not prepared...So the secret here is to combine inner work AND action together so that action becomes the tridimensional expression of the inner creation. (By the way, this encouraged us to call our NLP, ethical NLP, and to integrate Neuro-Semantics and other disciplines as well so it was more complete. The hope was to show that all these techniques are like surgical tools, powerful and precise instruments that can be used to save a life or injure one depending on the ethics and intent of the user.)

Both phases of the creation—the internal and the action—are important, both the meanings and the performance. Where do you tend to have more trouble? What do you need to do most?

THE QUESTIONS OF CREATION

(Review the questions of the seven steps)

- When you think of your vision, which of your beliefs are useless?
- If you could change one belief, which would it be?
- Are you absolutely sure about the truth of that belief? Are there moments in which it is not true?
- When did it start? How has it been validated? How could it be proven wrong?
- What would be more useful for you to believe and think instead?
- What are the beliefs of people who have reached objectives similar to yours? What do they believe? Who is like what you want to become? Imagine being able to have their beliefs. What would change? How would your relationships, your moods and your behaviors change?
- Have you ever felt that way? When?
- What could you start doing today to become what you want to become?
- What resources and help will you need? Who could help you?
- What new capacities will you need to develop?

- What will you do tomorrow? The day after tomorrow? In a week? A month?

SOLIDIFICATION

An object will remain in uniform motion in a straight line unless acted upon by an external force.

—Newton's first law

"Something has changed. I have been dating Robert for two months. The first time that we went out, he received three consecutive calls from his office and spent more than an hour on the phone. I thought of the old Sarah, of how she would have reacted. But now I did not feel diminished; actually I almost laughed. By the way, I even got the promotion!"

Sarah no longer believes that life has been stingy with her and that look of angry resignation is gone from her face. Even her skin is more luminous. She has a beautiful smile, and she gives it happily to whomever she meets. This is her new way of thinking—of being.

THE HIGHWAYS OF THE MIND

Are you thinking that you're too old for change? This is not a valid excuse. Neuroscience has amply documented the capacity of the human brain to design new patterns, new combinations of nerve cells and neurotransmitters in response to new stimuli. And this does not happen only in infancy but is possible at any age.

For change to last in time though, the new beliefs and behaviors must be reinforced and solidified.

What happens if this phase is skipped? It is very probable that the results obtained will not last and that the old habits will return. To paraphrase Newton, if we take away the stimulus too soon, the uniform straight line (or the old way) will continue indefinitely.

For Sarah, the belief "I'm ugly" was a true and real highway of the mind. Such a thought was formed by synapses and neuronal connections, used millions of times for years and years. Every time Sarah heard it from others, and all the times she said it to herself, validated it.

Exactly like dopamine and pleasure, even here, the more the thought pattern is repeated and the more synapses are formed, the more it becomes habitual.

When we create a change, we give life to new neuro- connections which are only small paths through the woods if compared to a highway of old habits.

Bruce Wexler, internationally renowned neuroscientist and author of *Brain and Culture,* affirms that to have success in change, it is necessary to have a big dose of concentration and an intense and uninterrupted repetition of the new behavior because usually it means fighting deep programming. Our brain, in fact, is programmed to save energy for the important functions like breathing and coordination of movements, and because the old habits require less energy, they tend to return.

To accomplish this, constant reinforcement of the neuro-connections is necessary until they become the preferred circuits and the old dysfunctional automatic ones, used less and less, shrink into small lanes.

It is at this point that new habits are formed and that we are not so at risk of relapse. It is here that Sarah, even when faced with a river of phone calls, does not feel diminished.

The fact that, in order to solidify change, it is necessary to create new habits is not a new concept. Aristotle sustained that virtues were the result of good habits cultivated over time. William James, the father of American psychology, at the beginning of the last century, wrote that habits are fundamental components of human psychology.

CELEBRATE RESULTS

To create new habits means then to reinforce the new functional neuroconnections to our objectives. But how can we?

The answer is simple: by using the mechanism of dopamine to our advantage! We must make new thoughts and behaviors seductive by associating pleasure with them (and/or distancing them from pain) and rewarding them until they eventually become automatic.

Attention! The reward must be immediate. We cannot wait until we reach the finish line to get paid, otherwise our neuronal system won't recognize that what we are doing is gratifying and we won't get the push we need from dopamine. To renounce French fries may not be very pleasant, but it may be if we start to lose a few pounds. Josh, for example, learned to be thrilled with each small success.

And you? Do you take the time to celebrate even the smallest results, or are you so focused on defects that you tend to see only what is not working?

We all have need for reassurance that we are improving, that we are making it. In psychology, this is known as positive reinforcement, and it does not work just with humans but also with animals. Every time we receive gratification because we are closer to our objective, our new behavior is reinforced.

The problem is that often we are such perfectionists that our small successes are not seen as successes so are not even taken into consideration. They are not validated and, consequently, the new behavior isn't reinforced at all.

If this is what it's like for you, you will find an exercise made just for you at the end of this chapter. It will teach you to celebrate daily every small success. To do it, you will need to redefine your idea of success because it is only with constant positive reinforcement that we can amplify our new results and solidify them.

What is success for you? When do you realize that you are successful at something? What has to happen for you to be happy about your success, to enjoy it and to congratulate yourself?

Another important aid for the solidification phase is to be able to count on someone who will encourage you to continue the change. Often, unfortunately, the opposite occurs and the people around us, afraid of the change in you, try to put obstacles in your way. If we want to facilitate the change, it is good to create a favorable environment so we won't have to count only on ourselves. In the transformation tools, you will find a section dedicated to this aspect and on how to form support groups.

THE CRITIC'S HAT

Once we have constructed a stable base through continued validation, the new pattern is solid enough to be tested. It is the moment to put on the critic's hat and to examine the new pattern to discover any weak points and those that can still be improved.

The idea is not to destroy the work that we have done but to do some real quality control as if you had to test the safety of an airplane before taking off.

Here we are again in a dance between emotion (the celebration of validation) and rationality (the critical part). Once again we are working the right brain (the vision) and the left brain (strategy and reasoning).

QUESTIONS OF SOLIDIFICATION

- How much do you have to practice a new way of thinking/behaving before it becomes automatic? Are you willing to do that?
- Have you associated pain with not doing it?
- What are the rewards for each of your small successes?
- How could you improve your results even more?
- Do you have the support of others? Who?
- If you don't have the support of others, how could you create it?
- If you do have the support of others, is it the type of support that you need? If it is not, what type of help would you like? Have you clearly asked for it from the people around you? In what other way could you communicate it even better?

A DAILY APPLAUSE

Write in your diary at least one thing a day that you consider a small or big success. It is important that the successes are of any type, not just working. They can be to have cooked a good meal, to have helped a stranger, to have listened to a friend...once you have written your success, give yourself an applause and find a way to celebrate. Be creative!

CHAPTER 7

TOOLS FOR
TRANSFORMATION

*A mother teaches her child with love and
patience until he has learned. Be a mother and
teach your mind to have positive thoughts and
to let go of worries. That way, when your mind
needs peace, it will obey you.*

*—Brahma Kumaris from
Reflections for A Better World*

Until we have stabilized the desired change, it is necessary to
use some tools with consistency and discipline to reinforce
the new sequence of beliefs, emotions, behaviors and habits.
Even if consistency and discipline are two words that we hate,
they are necessary. To obtain results we must train ourselves
with tenacity, exactly as if we were training our breathing and
muscles for a marathon.

Certainly, all of that can be looked upon as a sacrifice, especially at the beginning of the journey, but could not the meaning of the word sacrifice make it sacred? When we sacrifice the pleasure of the cigarette in exchange for our health or give up an afternoon of shopping to invest the time and money for our personal growth and spend an evening designing the map of our vision, does it not mean that we are making our time, our thoughts and our actions sacred?

To the woman who said enthusiastically to Beethoven after a concert, "How I wish that God had given me the same genius as he gave you; I would be so happy," the musician responded, "It's not genius, Madam. All you have to do is exercise for eight hours a day for forty years and you will be good like me."

And the explanation of Einstein, when he was asked the secret of his talent, was "One percent inspiration, ninety-nine percent perspiration!"

Even in all the traditional and ancient teachings, we find concepts of determination, perseverance, sacrifice and discipline. In Tibetan Buddhism, for example, for centuries, monks have dedicated hours and hours of their day studying and meditating. In Hinduism, they practice tapas, which are not only Spanish delicacies as Fabio, a participant in our course, thought. No, tapas are the austerities of silence and fasting and serve to stop letting ourselves be dominated by mental wandering and to progress in spiritual growth.

How can we, in the twenty-first century, train for complete realization? What tools do we have at our disposition?

In this chapter, we will find a variety of tools. The idea is to offer a choice of practices and suggestions that can sustain you during the change.

It's clear that these tools can't do everything for you, but, if you use them with regularity, they will be of great help.

Some are techniques, like the breathing methods.

Others are suggestions regarding physical exercise, correct diet and support groups that have worked for thousands of people throughout the world. Once these life-styles become our way of being, change has happened. However, it is very important to train ourselves to put them into action every single day.

In general, there are procedures and ideas that work together systematically and the confines between them are very fine. In every case, if you insert them in your daily routine, they will bring new ways of being. Some may suggest you meditate in silence in a cave for eight hours a day, but I have the idea that this practice may be unthinkable in your life. The tools that you find in this chapter, however, are very simple and can be done at any time.

THE MAGIC OF WORDS

> *The Sufi tell us to speak only when our words have passed through three gates. At the first gate, we ask ourselves, "Are these words true?" If they are, we'll let them pass. If they're not, we send them back. At the second gate, we ask ourselves if they are necessary. At the last gate, we ask if they are kind.*
>
> —*Eknath Easwaran*

Why does an ounce of butter weight gain more than an ounce of salad? The answer is obvious—butter and salad contain a different number of calories. Calories are energy stored in food. What we eat has a different effect on our body depending on the amount of energy, or calories, that it contains.

Have you ever thought that even words contain calories? You don't believe it? Yet, that's how it is. Depending on the stored energy in our words, they have different values and different effect on our emotions. Our way of speaking influences our mood, our beliefs, our perception of reality and even our behavior. Have you ever checked the calories in your words?

The ancient Vedas pay a lot of attention to the use of words, both in conversation with others and with ourselves. One of the practices that has been recommended for more than four thousand years is to repeat, even in silence, the name of the divine as often as you can so that your thoughts will go in that direction.

It is said that Swami Muktananda, a famous Indian mystic was explaining the power of word to a crowd when a young man protested loudly, "How stupid this is! They are only words! Do you think that, if I say bread-bread-bread in continuation, I will make my stomach full?"

The holy man stood and shook his finger threateningly. "Sit down, stupid idiot!" The young man went on a rampage, became very red, with veins in his neck swollen and, trembling with anger, answered, "You are a holy man and yet you would talk to me like that?" The guru smiled sweetly and said, "But, Sir. I don't understand. You heard yourself called idiot only once and look at the reaction that this simple word produced in your body. Don't you think repeating the name of the divine for hours and hours would have some effect?"

THE LINGUISTIC DIET

How would we change our life if we constantly followed a linguistic diet based on respect, love and appreciation, not only applied to that which we say to others aloud, but also and, above all, that which we say to ourselves during our interior dialogues?

How often do we say the words blessing and curse?

For people today, the words don't seem to count much; how much of it have we thought about? And how many times have we said something to take it back shortly after, without worrying if our words have hurt someone?

According to antique teachings, it did not used to be this way. In various traditions, Jewish, Christian and Asian, the word was heavy with meaning, as if it was a real thing and almost tangible.

John writes in the Bible, "In the beginning, there was the word, and the word was God and the word was made flesh." In other words, it is the word that gives life to actions.

* * *

When we met Sarah and we listened to her speak, we could not help but notice how she described her perception of herself: I'm ugly and unlucky. Everything good happens to other people (and, in particular, to my sister Carmen). I'm angry with the world because nothing good ever happens to me (no one, not men or even my boss, ever gives me what I deserve). These words were the script of her life.

A few days later, at the same course, we met Lenny, her boss, a robust man in his fifties with serious problems of hypertension and insomnia. Listening to the metaphors that he used to tell his story, I wondered how long his heart would hold out. The hypertension and the insomnia did not surprise me at all. I would have been surprised if he had been in good health. For him, work was a battlefield, the competition was an enemy to annihilate and the monthly budget was a fight to the death. If you think I'm exaggerating, there really are trainers out there who incite salesmen with, "You are cave men and, every morning, you go hunt your food. You will return beaten or winners; so any means is legal." Would you want to be one of their clients?

We Don't Describe the World That We See,
But We See the World That We Describe

All of us use a certain language to describe our experiences. In this way, we begin to create metaphors that guide our life, and it is through stories that we tell ourselves that we communicate with ourselves and with others. These mechanisms are, by now, true and real habits and, in most cases, we aren't even aware of the effects that they have on our lives, our work, our relationships and our well-being.

What are your metaphors? What kind of stories do you tell? Are these stories that teach or a victim's stories without hope? How did your day go? Was it as smooth as silk or was it an obstacle course? The stories that we tell become the script of our lives. If we convince ourselves that we are everybody's target and that everyone is out to get us, before long we will start to behave in such a way that it will be true.

Words make thoughts real so we must choose them very carefully, as we do when choosing calories in food on the supermarket shelf. We do not describe the world that we see, but we see the world that we describe.

Language has the magical capacity to alter our perception. We think through words and these same words have the power of imprisoning us or letting us free. Because of this, changing language will change your life.

During the course, we asked Sarah to choose a new way to of telling the story of her life. It would mean transforming negative thoughts and words into something more empowering, to find a new story that induces more positive and functional moods. Sarah thought for a bit and then answered, "I got it! My language may be that I'm not very pretty but I might be likable."

Well, this is not exactly what I was looking for…

At that time, her beliefs were so rooted that Sarah still had to work hard to recognize it and needed help to dig more deeply in the axis of awareness before she could make room for a new way of thinking. We suggested that she take a tape recorder with her and record her words. If we pay attention to how we speak, we will discover a lot about ourselves.

When we met Sarah a few weeks later, she had realized on her own how many times she repeated the same phrases. "I'm so ugly, who would ever want me? Nothing good ever happens to me." We did not have to do anything else. Sarah now knew that this kind of language was not good. She had reached the time to change her linguistic diet.

We helped her choose some phrases that could become her daily nutrition. We elaborated together, with precision, to put together a diet, and the result was part of the change that you read about in the earlier chapters. First timidly, then with more conviction, Sarah finally began to affirm to herself and to the world that she was an attractive woman, full of excellent qualities and that every day is rich with positive aspects. You only need to know how to grab them.

"At the beginning, I had difficulty believing it," she told us, "and it seemed that I was almost lying. But, then, as the days went by, I began to notice that I do have those qualities and that life does have gifts even for me. It's strange; I would never allow anyone else to call me ugly, fat, stupid and unlucky. Why did I do it so long to myself?"

Seeds for the Future

The linguistic diet is not made of lies about the present but of seeds for the future.

In the beginning, these seeds produce only small buds, and, if we are impatient and frustrated, we will yank them off because they are not exactly the result that we wanted to achieve. We'll have to start all over again. But if we are patient and continue to water, or actually repeatedly use the new language, in the end, the fruit that we desire will ripen.

Obviously, this process does not mean negating reality. If I don't have money to pay the rent, it won't help much to say that my bank account is prosperous. Probably, I'd end up in the street by doing that.

In that case, it is more useful to affirm that I have all the capacity necessary to create a new activity.

By using your own language, in fact, we promote new neuro-connections that give life to perception, moods and new actions. This is the magic of words. Exactly as the negative conditionings are rooted in our minds through constant repetition (look at mine: "Go slow!") or through emotionally charged events (for example, being refused in love, feeling judged insufficient or being hollered at in public), using the same factors, which are the repetition and emotional intensity, we can produce new moods, thoughts and behaviors. But, this time, they will work toward our objectives and will create a bridge to get to our desired future.

We can compare it to a medicine made of words. It is said in ancient Chinese that there are two kinds of doctors. The first cures with herbs; the second—much more elite and powerful—cures with words.

As we gradually modify our language, even if it does not change our life, it will definitely change the way we perceive it.

YOUR STORIES

Take a moment to analyze the stories that you tell yourself, the metaphors and the words that you mostly use at home and at work.

- What is work like for you?

- What is the story that you tell about it?
- Do you have to be careful of low blows? Do you think work is a long hard staircase or a great experiment? Or maybe a playground?
- What do you say about sentimental relationships?
- Does marriage mean death for love? Is it a well-kept garden where we plant new seeds every day and take the time to water them?
- And what do you think of life?
- Is it a tragic film where all the bad luck falls on you? Is it a love story where the heroine is waiting for her Prince Charming to save her (or the hero in search of a Princess to take care of) ? Maybe it's a comedy or a thriller full of anxiety.

Check the answers that you gave during the exercise about your stories.

Are they functional? Do they help you to be calm? Do they help you develop your talents and your abilities? Do they make the world (your personal world and your work world) a better place for you and others? If any answer is no, you can start a new diet and build new metaphors!

My New Diet

Reread your answers on the exploration of the matrix. What are your most recurring negative thoughts/ beliefs?

If you are not yet aware of them, listen! Register every time you talk on the phone or with friends and listen to how you describe your day, your history and your life.

Once you know the phrases that you use to put yourself down, to boycott or victimize yourself and to blame others, banish them from your diet!

Make a list of new thoughts to counterbalance the negative ones, that motivate you and that induce a state of mind with more potentiality. Here are some examples:

- I am not capable/I cannot do it—becomes—I have the capacity to do what I want to.
- I don't deserve anything in life—becomes—I deserve the best.
- Nothing ever goes right for me—becomes—my life is a series of pleasant surprises.
- Marriage is the death of love—becomes—marriage is a beautiful and passionate adventure.
- I am not ok and it's difficult to change—becomes—I am ok exactly as I am and can change easily.

These are examples and are very general. It is very important that you build the new empowering phrases in a personalized way, with your own words in a way that is good for you.

When you have made the list of new phrases, choose three, write them more that once in your diary, learn them by heart and repeat them at least seven times a day for at least twenty-one days. When you have finished, you can do the same with other phrases as often as necessary.

WHERE IS YOUR FOCUS?

> *A reason why so few of us achieve what we really want is that we don't manage our focus, and, in this way, we don't ever focus on our power. The majority of people live their entire life without deciding to excel in something in particular.*
>
> —*Anthony Robbins*

Have you ever experienced a moment of extreme clarity? A moment in which your whole concentration was on one thing, when you felt pushed by a flow and you knew exactly what to do?

Focus has been defined as a key to success in life and business and is decidedly indispensable in reaching your vision. Athletes often talk of their focus on an objective and the fact of being "in the zone", where everything else disappears.

The psychologist Mihaly Csikszentmihalyi conducted a research study for years on the phenomenon of flow, the state in which it feels effortless because we are totally immersed in what we are doing.

"I know what that means. I love to climb mountains and, in those moments, I feel exactly like that. Sometimes I find myself doing hikes so difficult that, later on, even I can't imagine how I did it. But when I am there, I feel a great energy and I have great clarity on which my next step must come from. Sarah is flabbergasted with herself. Most of us have had similar experiences, often in the context of a sport or hobby. It is in these moments that we have access to the state of flow, when we are at the height of our potential, and, if there is a possibility, a glimmer of hope for success, it is at that moment that we will achieve it. Often, it's not about lowering the difficulty of the challenge but of raising our capacity to focus. In the section dedicated to meditation and breathing, you will find exercises to train your concentration.

Even in shamanic psychology, teachings are found regarding the importance of focus. This concept in the tribal traditions is often symbolized by big cats like puma, lions and tigers. All that is needed is to observe the behavior of these mammals when hunting and the analogy is quickly evident: the animal has a clear objective and is very motivated. It needs to be able to feed itself and its children. Then it goes into action. Have you ever had occasion to observe a cat following its prey? Every single muscle extends and contracts elegantly and every part of its body is in motion—everything but its head. The eyes and the head of cats always remain completely fixed on the objective as if it were tied to it by an invisible string and follow every single movement of the prey. If it takes its attention away for only a second, it would end up moving their powerful muscles in another direction wasting time, strength and energy. And it would probably end up without food.

This is the ability that it takes to train—the capacity to keep our interior eye fixed on an objective allows the maximization of the powers of mind and body.

On the journey toward our vision, if the flame of passion is the fuel, focusing is the steering wheel. Both are required.

In reality, even we humans are able to focus our thoughts and actions. But, unfortunately, we are used to using this capacity to the contrary, in its dysfunctional form. As soon as we meet obstacles, conditionings are activated. The objective that, until yesterday, was reachable—maybe not easily, but feasibly—suddenly becomes unrealistic. We begin to focus on how difficult it will be to succeed and on the thousands of potential risks. We are great at believing in the old programming of the matrix which say, "I am not capable. It takes too much time, money. I'm too old/young. Imagine what people will say. I'll look ridiculous. I won't make it." If something can go wrong, we will visualize it and direct our energies there. And we will be sure to repeat this as much as we can. Every time we think of our dream, the visualization of all the risks takes off and there goes our concentration and our focus.

"It's like being in front of a very steep wall; I begin to concentrate on everything that may go wrong.... Well, I think I would have stopped climbing a long time ago..." Sarah thought and smiled. By now, for her, the wheels of change have begun to spin in the right direction.

THE STRUCTURE OF OPTIMISM

The pessimist sees difficulty in every opportunity; the optimist sees opportunity in every difficulty.

—*Winston Churchill*

Glass half full or half empty? How important is it to see it one way or the other? And what difference does it make in daily life?

In 1981, a group of researchers led by the scientist R. G. M. Morris did an experiment that gives us the idea of the importance of optimism. In the first phase, some mice were put in a tub of opaque liquid, similar to milk. To remain afloat, the animals had to swim. Seeing that it was a very tiring and almost impossible task, all of them gave up in a short time. They decided to let themselves drown. Only then did the scientists save them. Then a second group of mice was put in a similar tub. The only difference was that the scientists had inserted a small island at the center, a kind of oasis where the animals could rest. Thanks to the island, the second group was able to stay in the deep water for a long time. They had understood that they could do it. In a third phase of the experiment, both groups of mice were united in the first tub without the island of safety. What do you think happened? Did both groups have the same behavior? Did they get the same results this time seeing that they were in the same situation? Absolutely not. Even if they all had identical environmental conditions and none had the benefit of the oasis for rest, the mice from the first group did not try to save themselves giving up quickly while the second group demonstrated a resistance three times higher in terms of the time that they continued to swim and in terms of the distance that they were able to swim in the liquid.

What was the difference that made the difference? It was nothing external. It was only their inner attitude. And these are just mice...

Even if the platform was not there anymore, the hope and positive expectations facilitated the second group giving them help that was concrete and tangible. In the first group though, the expectation of not surviving brought them to desperation and to giving up.

Which group do you want to join?

WHAT IS NOT WORKING?

Maybe thanks to his experience as an auditor, Lenny, Sarah's boss, had a unique talent of capturing every possible thing that could go wrong. And he never failed to remember all the occasions in which the worst had actually happened. His typical question was: what's not working today? Sometimes the question was asked in a different version: What could go wrong? What other risks might there be? And so on...

If this approach was useful when he had to check contracts, balance sheets and defective merchandise, it certainly was not the optimal lens through which to view his life and his behavior with others. Our first suggestion was to save these questions for the times when he really needed it, and, for the rest, to transform it into: What is working today?

What Lenny still did not understand was that negative thoughts and emotions damage the cardiovascular system. Various studies have demonstrated that emotions like fear, anger and stress, besides causing an increase in blood pressure and heart rate straining the heart, also induce an increase in cortisol and adrenaline, two chemical substances that become extremely dangerous when they exceed a certain threshold.

The good news is that through positive emotions, like joy and love, we have the possibility to repair this kind of damage. And this is not just a new age assertion but the actual results of the most recent scientific research.

Barbara Fredrickson, of the University of Michigan, has conducted many experiments in which certain emotions were induced in people through the viewing of emotion-evoking short films. After having shown the volunteers sad, violent and horror films, her team checked the cardiovascular system. All participants showed symptoms of stress, such as an increase in blood pressure and heart rate and cardiovascular constriction.

Then the same people were divided into three groups. The first group was shown funny films or those with positive themes. The second group was shown neutral films. The third group was not shown any more films but simply used the time to recover from the stress.

At the end of the experiment, the volunteers were all re-examined. Only the people in the first group, those who watched films with positive emotions, had readings back to normal while the other two groups were still very altered.

Still far from solving the simple metaphor of the glass half full or half empty, the idea of optimism and, in general, the influence of positive emotions on our psycho-nervous system, has interested scientists from all over the world. In the United States and Australia, many of the most important universities have promoted further research.

The results seem to confirm that positive emotions increase intellectual capacity and optimistic people are more creative and capable of resolving problems. In fact, all of the experiments conducted by Fredrickson, by Alice Isen of Cornell University, Seligman and hundreds of their colleagues have demonstrated that optimistic people have better health and more capacity when confronted with challenges and difficulty because they are more proactive, flexible and open to information.

Among the many interesting experiments, there are a couple that made Lenny wonder about the effectiveness of his proverbial pessimism. The first is reported by Mihaly Csikszentmihalyi and regards the corporate world. Certain researchers have followed and measured work activity, performance and productivity of 272 workers for eighteen months. The positive optimistic people reported evaluations (and salaries) decidedly better than the others. The study was from the Mayo Clinic in Rochester, Minnesota, where a study of 839 patients was able to conclude that optimists live 19 percent longer.

I'm not sure which of the two motivations was more important for Lenny, if it was to get better work results or to live longer. At that time, he was one of those people very attached to financial success.

He loved to define himself as a conductor and had always considered pessimism as a motivator for success because, through the technique of considering everything a catastrophe, it gave the illusion that he could keep everything under control. In his attempt to manage the unforeseen events in life, he had taught his body to live in a constant state of psychological and muscular tension.

Now he was afraid that relaxing would make him lose everything, but, at the same time, he knew he could not go on like this. He was gradually generating the motivation to change. But how could he unlearn seeing everything from the negative side?

Can You Learn Optimism?

In the paragraph dedicated to instructions on the correct functioning of the mind, we examined the cognitive distortions or errors in thinking that determine unhappiness, the 3Ps, permanence, personalization and pervasion.

When we let one of these 3Ps enter our psyche, it's a little like activating a virus in our computer. It sends our system into tilt and takes up all the space possible taking with it the power of self-determination.

It's enough to invert these mental processes to obtain the structure of optimism.

"In our department, there is always a crisis and, unfortunately, there is not a day when I can fully count on my staff. How can I ever be calm?" Lenny asked, worried during our first meeting.

Considerations like this, in terms of "never" and "always," indicate that we are extremely pessimistic.

Too often we fall into the trap of believing that negative things that happen (or better yet, could happen) are permanent and that the crisis will last forever. If, as Buddhism teaches us, everything (in general) has a beginning and an end and nothing is permanent, why should negative events be?

When something goes badly, it's natural to be upset. Sometimes life's difficulties are like a punch in the stomach; they burn and they hurt. For some, the pain disappears quickly while others need more time. Still others are convinced that the pain is permanent and, for them, it is much harder to get over it.

Happy people are not necessarily those who have the best, but they are those who look for the best in what they have.

The substantial difference between a pessimist and an optimist is that the pessimist thinks that things are always going badly and that they'll never have what they want. The optimist knows that, every once in a while, things may go badly and we may not get what we want, but they don't focus on it.

With a good motivation and constant training, optimism can be learned. When Lenny started to ask, "Is it really always like this? Is there always a crisis? Is it true that I can never trust my colleagues? Really never?" he then realized that often his way of thinking did not correspond to reality. For example, if it was true that the area where he worked was going through a difficult moment, there were just as many areas where there was still a good profit. Some of his colleagues were new and did not completely understand the work yet, so, sometimes, they made errors. Others, however, among whom Sarah, completed their work tasks accurately. Was it true that he could not ever count on his staff? No, in fact, the opposite was true.

Another error in thinking that Lenny used to make was to personalize everything that happened in his life. Two co-workers chatted at the coffee machine? Surely they were talking badly about him. A client did not confirm their order? Surely it was because of him. The maid forgot to pick up his clothes at the dry cleaner? It was to spite him.

When we suggested that he ask himself, 'What proof do I have that it's really like that? What other interpretations could there be?' his habit of personalizing everything eased.

The third P is about pervasiveness, or allowing negative events or their memory to affect other areas. If permanence is about time, then pervasiveness is about space. Needless to say, Lenny was a champion at this. A worker made an error? "Nothing works here" was his conclusion. Only one client did not pay on time? Right away, he thought, "The clients are not paying any more." A contract did not get signed? "My life is a failure," he deduced.

The question that helped him get out of this pattern was: What does that have to do with this? How does one colleague's error mean that the whole company does not work and that all the employees are incompetent?

WANT TO LEARN THE 3PS POSITIVELY?

Begin to believe that everything good has to do with you. Be joyous when the day is sunny. Be joyous viewing a beautiful landscape or listening to beautiful music. Be joyous at passerby's smile. Be joyous when someone helps you unexpectedly. That sun, that panorama, that music, that smile and that help are there just for you!

Let the experience of a positive moment pervade your whole day and grow it to the whole week. Notice how beauty and grace become permanent in your life. Begin to consider difficult moments as nothing more than clouds that are in the sky for a while. Above the clouds, the sky is always blue and clear.

Make the memory of a success in one area of your life, an objective achieved, become a safety island, an area of restoration, just like in Morris' experiment. It will give you the strength to succeed in other areas as well.

To train for this, we asked Lenny to make a list of the aspects of his life and work that gave him joy and that aroused positive emotions.

In the beginning, it was not easy and he did not know what to write. "I challenge anyone to do it after concentrating on what does not work for fifty years!" he ironically commented. But then he did it and created a list of almost two pages that ranged from playing with Goofy, his Black Lab, to sipping a cocktail while watching a sunset at the beach. We then suggested that he read the list at least twenty times a day so that the positive feelings would pervade his day. In a short time, Lenny noticed his tension faded. His brain could not process fear and appreciation at the same time. So the list of things he appreciated, more than being practice for optimism, was also an efficient tool against stress.

"When faced with problems, I used to react automatically thinking that there would be a disaster. Now I think that there must be a solution. It's not always the best outcome, but something good happens, one way or the other. And I'm learning to see it that way," admits Lenny.

Optimism can be defined as the art of responding positively to life and sustains that it is the fuel for our spirit. Without this tool at our disposition, how can we reach our vision?

Being optimistic means having faith in the bounty that sustains the universe, having trust that this bounty will eventually manifest itself and will show care, respect and attention for others.

We're talking about faith, hope and love.

THE LIST OF APPRECIATION

Make a list of at least twenty things that you appreciate including at least six for which you are grateful. You can include things about your body, your personality, qualities of your character. They can be parts of your life, of your work. They can be about people in your life that are dear to you, friends or family. It can include places, animals, food, music, people that you love and that you think make you happy.

Read this list at least five times a day and keep it with you.

If you feel that you are falling into the 3P trap, read the list before asking yourself:

- How am I personalizing this situation?
- How am I imagining it to be permanent?

- How am I generalizing (allowing it to pervade other areas)?

SPIRITUALITY AND FAITH

All human beings by nature are Buddha—like ice for nature is water. Without water, there is no ice. Without human beings, there is no Buddha.

—Hakun Ekaku

"Honestly, it is difficult for me to believe in God. I'm certainly not one to go to mass on Sunday. I define myself pretty much an atheist. What proof do we have that God exists? And what does it matter in my life anyway?" Lenny seemed upset about this topic.

Many people, by reaction, have refused the religion imposed by society or their parents. But, together with the rigid rules of religion, they have rejected spirituality as well and taken refuge in pure materialism negating a fundamental need of human beings. It's a bit like throwing the baby out with the dirty bath water. Religions can be a path toward spirituality, but, if they blur the integral flow, they end up becoming an obstacle to transcendence. Spirituality goes far beyond the dogmas of organized religion.

FUNDAMENTAL HUMAN QUALITIES

If you go to fifty different countries, you will find fifty different images and names for God depending on the culture and local customs, but if we could distill the concept of God and recreate it based on qualities, what would it be? Would it be hate, mistrust, greed, insensibility, selfishness and falsehoods? Or would there be more kindness, gentleness, compassion, love, trust, generosity, availability and truth?

Aren't these last characteristics of universal humans that we can find at almost every latitude and longitude? Are they not the actual qualities of the human soul—at least of its bright side?

The Dalai Lama sustains that, even though it's natural that religious dogma can be shared only by part of humanity, the qualities are universal. Every member of the human family needs to be able to fully develop their own potentialities and to live a life with more significance and more joy.

So it does not matter if, like Lenny, we declare ourselves atheist or if we are Buddhists, Christians, Jewish or Muslim. When we speak of spiritual qualities, we are actually speaking of fundamental human qualities.

I must admit that my spiritual journey is quite bizarre. I come from an Italian Catholic family and, living my childhood in Africa, I was exposed to a variety of forms of that which we might define as "soulism," which we will discuss in the section dedicated to Mother Earth. For these ancient religions, the idea was not only that nature is alive but that spirits, too, live here. This experience, along with my future study of Native Americans, gave me a great respect for nature and all its forms of life. As an adolescent, I was strongly drawn to Eastern religion. During various trips between India and Nepal, I was fascinated by Sanatana Dharma, which in Sanskrit means "eternal law" and is known to most as Hinduism. I would not know how to define a religion, either as a philosophy or as a way of living, but, maybe because it's been developed over thousands of years and does not come from a single source, what strikes me is its great capacity to *include* more than *exclude*. In my experience in this field, I was never approached in an attempt to convert me, but I was drawn to accept a variety of archetypical divinities. The result for me was a great lesson in tolerance and liberty and, at the same time, a clear spiritual discipline to embrace.

Later, I had the possibility to understand quite deeply various forms of Buddhism, first Tibetan then Chinese, Japanese and finally Thai. It's difficult for me to summarize in a few words all that these studies and the relative experiences have given me, but I can definitely confirm that, when I confronted the teachings that I received with that of my psychological and cognitive formation, I discovered that most of the principals were the same! For example, are not spiritual qualities similar to those promoted by the movement of human potential by Maslow—who, by the way, defined himself as atheist—and of the psychology of self-actualization? Therefore, can't we confidently affirm that our spiritual path is nothing more than a journey toward the full realization of our best parts?

"Yes, it certainly is," admits Lenny thoughtfully. "With these concepts, it's easier for me to know what to do, but when it comes to faith, I struggle. Maybe that's why I can't seem to have a religious view of life."

The psychiatrist Carl Gustav Jung, who extensively studied Buddhist philosophy and spiritual dimensions, in a book titled *Modern Man in Search of the Soul* wrote, "During the last thirty years, people of every part of Earth have come to consult with me. I have healed many hundreds of the ill. Among all of those who were in the second half of life, those who were over thirty-five years of age, there was not even one whose problem did not have something to do with finding a religious view of life."

But what does it mean to find a spiritual view of life?

When, during a television interview, the anthropologist Mel Konner was asked why every population had a form of spirituality, why every culture sought God, he answered, "It's not God that man is always seeking; through spirituality, people are seeking enthusiasm for life and trying to understand what it really means to live."

Amma sustains that if human life is like a rough sea, spirituality is equivalent to knowing how to swim.

SPIRITUAL INTELLIGENCE

Many studies demonstrate how people of faith, regardless of which religion, are happier. Moreover, they are healthier in terms of their immune system and have forty per cent less chance of having high blood pressure and coronary problems. It is pretty much proven that a belief system that includes spiritual values helps confront challenges and improves their lives, so much so that, within the study of various types of intelligence, *spiritual intelligence* has been recognized.

In an article, Giampiero Cara, journalist, author and expert in the field, states: "According to the definition that experts of the International Institute of Transformation who are studying in the United States, spiritual intelligence allows us to use rational and emotional intelligence in a unified way to improve our life and that of all living things."[14]

Great political and spiritual leaders of the caliber of Gandhi, Mother Teresa, Martin Luther King and Nelson Mandela, to name a few, are (or were) gifted with great spiritual intelligence.

According to American researchers, in this decade and beyond, spiritual intelligence will be a determining factor for the success of a person. Why? Both rational and emotional intelligence need already-existing information to operate, while spiritual intelligence, based on awareness of spiritual laws on which the universe is founded, reflects the capacity to think beyond the confines of the known and then to perceive a higher truth. Therefore, it is only when these three types of

---

[14] Giampiero Cara, 'Discover Spiritual Intelligence': how much do you have?

intelligence work in unison and are guided by spiritual intelligence, that we are able to completely show our potential to the world…

Spiritual intelligence takes us beyond our own selves, toward that which Maslow defined as self-realization. It guides us to researching the reason for our life, helping us to distinguish the joy of happiness. It is a love relationship that nothing and no one can take away and that supports us when everything around us falls apart. This is what man has always sought.

Many years ago, in some part of the world, I heard someone use a beautiful metaphor: during life we are like astronauts that orbit around the Earth. We need to be connected to the base that tells us how to navigate and how to maneuver. And this connection helps us make better decisions and gives us strength. This thread of gold that connects us is the spiritual connection. When such a connection is missing or fades, we feel confused, lost, without a goal.

"It would be nice to feel this connection. But how can you have such an unshakable faith?" Lenny asked perplexed. He was very skeptical about this.

Many people believe that having faith is the same as not having doubts, so, if they have them, they convince themselves that they don't believe in anything. Instead, once again, it means to embrace the paradox. As Lauren Artress, Episcopal priest and honorary Canon of Grace Cathedral in San Francisco, sustains that to have faith mostly means to feel that something larger than we are is taking us over. It means believing that sooner or later we will be able to complete the purpose of our life and our vision, even if the route to get there is tortuous. Sometimes we are given a map, but, more often, we walk in complete darkness.

"I know that darkness well," whispered Lenny with a voice cracking with emotion. "When I was thirty, my wife died in a car accident. She was five months pregnant. I threw myself into work and tried in every way to keep everything under control, but, obviously, it was impossible."

Viktor Frankl observed that, among his companions, only those who have spiritual values and faith in their life were able to survive. Frankl was one of the first to write about psychoneuroimmunology. In one of his writings, you will read, "Whoever knows how close the connection between man's mind, courage and hope (or their absence) and the immune system status will understand that a sudden loss of hope and courage can have a deadly effect."

THE FORM OF GOD

"I was angry with God for taking Laura from me, and I only now understand that God is not someone who governs events. To ask how God could make certain things happen does not help or result in anything good. The correct question to ask yourself is, 'How can God help us and give us the strength to manage what happened? Life is made of marvelous moments and tragic losses, and the spiritual quality that I speak of can help to accept both.'" Lenny breathed and brought his hand to his heart that for so long had been closed.

You don't have to embrace a religion no matter what to develop faith and spiritual intelligence. It's obviously a personal choice. If you are a believer and are fine with that, continue that way. But even if you have not chosen a particular religion, that's fine too. Know that there are many ways to reach the divine if you want. Religions are only some of the ways, while spirituality is like a big umbrella that welcomes them all. It is their essence and transcends them at the same time.

Naturally God can take different names for different people. Some believe literally in a fatherly figure with a white beard that takes care of humanity. For others, it is a light, a spirit, a kind of theme that sustains the universe or a form of superior intelligence. Monotheistic religions represent him mostly in the masculine form while, in antiquity, often it was a female figure like the mother of the world from whom all have life. For some populations, there is no form, for others it is in the rocks, in the mountains, in the plants or in the animals. For yet others, it is within ourselves and the best part of ourselves to develop, a kind of ancient wisdom to draw from. In general, for everyone, when we connect to this essence, we experience a deep peace and we have the sensation of expanding ourselves and merging with the universe.

Personally, I cannot say that I have scientific proof that this Superior Intelligence (or however you choose to call it) exists, but I can definitely affirm that I have felt its presence over and over.

It has happened often in beautiful moments but also in the most difficult moments of my life.

A PRESENCE

"It's your mother on the phone." It was six in the morning when I heard an insistent sound but I could not decipher where it came from. I could not understand if it was in my dream or if it was real. I decided that it did not make a big difference, but I was wrong.

I tried hard to open even one eye and I saw John who was handing me the phone. His hands were shaking. He was very pale and his usual smile was spent. "Your father is dead," he said with a grave tone.

"Dead? How did he die? It's not possible. I saw him last night at supper and he was fine. Are you joking?"

He cannot answer. He has a tear tracing a line on his face.

I jump up. I feel a shock of adrenaline go through my body. "Hello. Mamma, what happened?" I was able to ask.

They had awoken shortly before. "I don't feel very well," my father had told her, but he was not even able to finish the phrase. A heart attack had killed him instantly.

What does one do in a moment like that? How does one behave? Unfortunately, school does not prepare us for events like this.

It was February of 2000, the day of my thirty-sixth birthday. I had arrived in Florence at my then fiancé John's house that same night. My plans had been different. I was going to stay in Milan a day longer, celebrate that evening in Bologna at my parents' house and get to Florence that evening, but, at the last minute, I pushed everything up one day. So the evening before, I ate with my parents and that day I was in Florence. Premonition? Pure coincidence?

Whom must I thank for this inspiration? Even though it was almost midnight and I had to still drive over the Apennines for more than a hundred kilometers, the last words that my father had said to me at the door were not "Go slowly" but "I'm very proud of you. I love you." I will always carry that with me in my heart. I love you too, Papa. And I am also proud of you.

Still in my pajamas, I went out in the garden and sat under my favorite tree. And there, in Mother Earth's lap, leaning on the trunk, I cried all my pain. Bit by bit, as I let the tears come, it was as if someone or something put balm on my wounds. "Everything will be fine," the leaves seemed to whisper. Everything is fine. Papa is well now.

"Do you want me to go with you?" John asked worriedly as soon as I went back in the house.

"No, thank you. I'd rather go alone." In an hour, or at the most two, I was at my mother's. Not only was my father dead but my mother was desperate.

Because of a series of coincidences, among which a strike of funeral home companies (really), we had to keep my father in the house for a whole day. And for a whole day, I was able to keep vigil for him. Maybe you'll think I'm crazy if I tell you that they were some of the sweetest and most tender times that I ever had. While I held his hand, I felt a deep peace. Of course, the human part of me was in pain, but there was a part of me that knew and felt that which I had only imagined intellectually earlier: Death does not exist. Of course, the physical body goes but there is something, maybe the thing we call the soul that remains. Just like the connection to people that we love but who are not here in the physical world any longer. And I still feel it. I have talked about this to many people who have had similar experiences as mine, and I discovered that I am not alone; it is actually quite common. And I'm not talking about spiritual séances or things like that. I'm talking about the famous thread of gold that unites us all, of an intelligence or superior order that watches over us.

Illusion? Self-convincing? Hope? Reality? But really, what does it matter? For me, the most important thing is that this gold filament works. In my experience, as in that of many others, to establish this connection induces me to open my heart and feel love and optimism because I know that I am guided and that everything that happens is for my own good and that, even if it is sometimes difficult to see the whole picture, I can always count on the wisdom of the universe and I am safe. And everything is good.

* * *

Obviously having a relationship with God (or however you want to call him) is like having a relationship with anyone else: we have to dedicate time. And, during this time, there are various things that we can do. Every spiritual tradition has teachings and techniques to bring us closer to God.

In the following paragraphs, we will talk about, nature, breathing, diet, contact with animals. They are all ways that can help us strengthen the golden thread and are areas so vast that a whole book could be written on each of these topics.

What I intend to offer here, and the same is true for the rest of the book, is a summary of my experiences, some of the practices that work for me and that have been tested by millions of people. And I know very well that there are many more—equally valid.

In general, the more often we focus our mind on that which for us is the Divine, the more we are encouraged to be more spiritual. This helps us establish relationships that are sincerer, to become more compassionate, to remember to honor life and to feel grateful for the simple fact of being alive. It fills us with strength and courage our dark moments. In other words, it makes us better people.

CREATE YOUR OWN SACRED SPACE

All over the world, millions of men and women of every religion have a small altar at home. Instead of limiting themselves by going to meet the divine in a cultish place once a week, these people have chosen, at least symbolically, to bring the divine into their daily lives. Each one honors what is sacred for them in their own way. They stand before their altar to receive nourishment, rediscover courage, love and faith and to remember who they are. The altar is even a physical representation of that which is sacred for them.

What do you consider sacred? What has a place on the altar of your life?

Find a place in your home where you can place your altar. It's not necessary that it's big. It could be a corner of your home office, the living room or your bedroom. And then create the base for the altar. A box covered with a cloth, a small table, a shelf or your bureau would be fine. Once you've decided on it, decorate it and make it special.

Sit silently for a few minutes and imagine what you want to put in this place.

What is divine for you? How will you represent it?

Let the ideas come: images, sacred objects, photos of people that have a deep significance for you.

Then put these things on the altar, one by one, paying attention to how you feel while you are doing it.

Every day, spend a few minutes in front of your altar, do what you need to do in order to reinforce your relationship with the divine and to evoke in you love and beauty. For example, you might want to light some incense, a candle, put some flowers, say a prayer or listen to sacred music.

These actions, together with watching an image or object that represents the divine, help to cultivate spiritual qualities. Like when we are away from home and look at photos of our loved one or our family and feel the love that we have for them, through these images of the divine and these ritualistic actions, we evoke in ourselves the spiritual connection.

When you feel down and need comfort or are simply looking for creativity or relaxation, go to your sacred space.

BREATH: A THREAD BETWEEN US AND INFINITY

> *There is a way to breathe that is inhibited and restrictive. But there is another way: a breath of love that leads you to infinity.*
>
> —*Rumi*

"Do I know the sound of my breath? No, I never noticed. But what does breathing have to do with change?"

A Zen student told his master that he had difficulty concentrating. The master told him to concentrate on his breathing. But the student complained, "Breathing is not very interesting." The master took the boy, pushed him into a tub of water and held his head under for a few seconds. When the boy came desperately to the surface to get air, the master asked, "So is breathing so uninteresting?"

In all ancient traditions, breathing is connected to the spirit.

For the Greeks, the spirit was Pneuma, the breath of life. For the Romans, it was Spiritus; for the Hindus, it was *Atman*, which means "God in the body." In the Koran, with the words *nafas* and *ruh*, "the breath and soul of Allah," breath is like a divine energy that regulates emotions and the equilibrium of the human body. In Hebrew, the name of God is YHWH. It is never pronounced. But if you try, the sound that would be produced would be similar to that of a breath.

In the second chapter of Genesis, God created the first human and "breathed in his nostrils the breath of life," and man became a living soul.

In one of the oldest books by the Yoga Kashmiri, the practitioner is instructed to breathe deeply so the spirit is nourished, and it is said that miracles of the yogi are principally due to breath control. Myth? Truth? The truth is that, by changing the way of breathing, we change the chemical composition of our blood and modify our emotions and mood.

Dan Brulé, pioneer in the study of breathing, explains, "The ways of breathing are like fingerprints, unique for each one of us and unique in every moment. The way you breathe when you are jealous or angry is different for the way you breathe when you are at peace with the world. The way you breathe when you work on a math problem is different from the way you breathe when you have an orgasm. Whatever problem you have, whatever challenges of the moment, there are certain ways to breathe that stimulate your symptoms of distress or even make them worse, while there are other ways of breathing that reduce and even eliminate them. There are even ways to breathe that produce deep states of peace, intuition and ecstasy."

A BRIDGE

Breathing is a perfect bridge between the conscious and the unconscious. It is one of the few bodily functions that we can consciously react to. If we want, we can speed up our breathing, slow it down, amplify it or deepen it. But it continues to work even when we don't worry about it. In this moment, as you are reading and your attention is elsewhere, your breathing continues to exist.

In other words, it is the only function that we cannot survive without for more than a few minutes. We can fast for days, even a month or more; we can go without drinking for about three days; we can go without sleep for over twenty-four hours without having any brain damage—but—we cannot go without breathing for more than three minutes!

Seventy-five percent of the toxins in our body are released by breathing. Recent studies have demonstrated that patients with heart disease and myocardial infarction who learn deep breathing significantly improve their long-term health.

Deep breathing is a full invigorating massage of the internal organs and abdominal muscles and is shown to be helpful in many cases of hypertension and anxiety.

In his handbook, on how to achieve excellent health, the celebrated author and doctor, Andrew Weil, puts breathing in first place affirming, "The only and most efficient technique for relaxation that I know is the conscious regulation of breathing. By simply focusing attention on breathing, and not doing anything to change it, you are on your way to relaxation."

Danger: Hold Your Breath!

On the contrary, the first reaction we have when confronted with something or someone we fear is to hold our breath. It's an ancient unconscious reaction that we've inherited from our hunter ancestors, a reaction that we can still see today in the actions of animals. Think about a wild animal sniffing danger. Its first reaction is to hold its breath and then decide whether to fake its own death, to escape or to attack. We, too, when confronted with the challenges of life, tend to hold our breath. By doing this, the rate of carbon dioxide in our blood increases causing a numbness of our senses which allows us to forget our fear. But we don't live in the forest any more. We don't have to defend ourselves from tigers with saber-like teeth like our ancestors did. The dangers we face now are more or less emotional. Now we try to defend ourselves from what we perceive as verbal aggression, existential disaster, from the sense of inadequacy and from the fear of being judged. And every single time that a similar thought arises, we automatically hold our breath. You don't believe it? The next time you drive too quickly past a police car, notice how you breathe…

The risk is to get used to holding our breathing capacities at a minimum, as if we had to continually protect ourselves from danger. By doing this, we constantly live with the sensation of not having enough.

Do you think you don't have enough time, money, love, friends and so on? Do your cells need oxygen?

It is only when we finally start breathing again and modify our breathing patterns that transformation can begin.

THE HANDBOOK OF BREATHING[15]

1. Every once in a while, during the day, pay attention to your breathing. Listen to it: take stock of it. You can do it at any moment—even if you're busy with other things.
2. Every once in a while, during the day, deepen your breathing. Take at least five deep breaths—ten would be better. You can do this at any moment even if you're busy doing other things.
3. When you breathe more deeply, do it in a relaxed way. You don't have to force it.
4. When you breathe more deeply, exhale in a relaxed way. Don't push the air out; let it out naturally.
5. Don't pause between breathing in and breathing out. Try to create a constant flow and relaxed inhaling and exhaling of air.
6. If you inhale through your nose, exhale through your nose. If you inhale through your mouth, exhale through your mouth. It's different from what you have heard but it's healthier.
7. Breathe imagining that your rib cage is an accordion, opening when you inhale and closing when you exhale.
8. Breathe slowly if you want to relax. Use a faster rhythm if you want to recharge.
9. If you're not in a very good mood (you're sad, distressed, anxious, nervous, or worried), exhale imagining that whatever you are feeling leaves and, when you inhale, joy, tranquility, peace and relaxation enter together with the air.

---

[15] From Milena Screm, "Breathing an Nature," *LifeGate,* January 14, 2004.

10. Find at least ten minutes a day to dedicate to yourself and to your breathing in complete tranquility. For ten minutes, lie down, breathe fully and let your whole body breathe, rest and regenerate.

"Mitakuye Oyain"(We Are All Connected)

If the trees are arms that hold up the sky, when we have cut the last tree, the sky will fall on top of us.

—*Old Indios song*

A few years ago, we helped a friend set up a series of meetings in Italy with two Peruvian shamans. Don Ramon is a *curandero* from the Andes while Don Alberto came from the Amazon forest. Neither had ever left their villages before this. We hosted them at our house when they arrived in Milan. At that time, we lived very close to the Duomo Cathedral, so we went out to take a walking tour of the city. We hadn't gone five hundred yards when we realized that both men were visibly disturbed. "But how can you live here?" they asked. "Pachamama (Mother Earth) is dead in the midst of all this cement. How do you recharge? Where do you get your energy from? Where do you find peace?" Great questions. Too bad the answers are so complicated. Maybe I should write a book, I thought.

Another shaman, this time African, Malidoma Patrice Somé, tells how, according to the Dagara, an indigenous population of the Burkina Faso, the divine is without words. It has no need to speak because true meaning is perceived instantly in a timeless awareness. In their population, there is a distinct hierarchy. The elements of nature, especially trees and plants, require the most respect because they have the most intelligence. In fact, they don't need words to communicate. In this way, they are closest to the divine and to the deep meaning that is behind language.[16]

The species after this classification is animals because they use only the absolute minimum of oral communication; their language is still close to the divine source. The last species is made up of those who need words to communicate because they are nothing more than a distant reflection of the original meaning: human beings.

Even the shamans of the Peruvian Amazon forest speak of the existence of beings invisible to the human eye that live in animals, plants, crystals, rocks and waterways. These beings, called Maninkari, teach the shaman all he needs to know and make sure that he develops all his power to its full potential.

According to tribal philosophy, every plant, hill, mountain and rock that was on the Earth before the coming of man, emits a subtle energy that has curative powers. Whether we are aware of it or not, there are all the necessary elements and principals necessary for healing in nature.

Nature is the fundamental basis for life even in our Western world as it is in the indigenous world and is still how it has been for thousands of years in every civilization, including that of our ancestors. For Native American Indians, *Mitakuye Oyasin* means "we are all connected," and this does not mean just animals but everything in nature.

Mother Earth does not give only oxygen for us to live, the food we eat or the water to quench our thirst and wash ourselves, but it also gives us a continuous well of energy and of serenity.

---

[16] From *The healing wisdom of Africa*, Malidoma Patrice Somé, The Meeting Place Editore, Vicenza 2000.

"Maybe this is why when I spend some time in the country, I feel better and less anxious?" Sally seemed very interested in this topic.

Personally, I believe that the implications that nature has on our health, even psychological, are much more than we imagine. For example, I live in the country and when I open the window, I see fields. I cannot help but notice how, in every season, the Earth presents well-defined characteristics and gives precise fruits. In spring, the fields are green, the wheat is still grass, the trees are in full bloom, the colors predominantly the pink and white of peaches and cherries. Then comes summer and everything becomes golden; the wheat matures and the buds swell until they bend. Next comes fall, the season of grapes and kiwi. The air fills with the perfume of moss and mushrooms, the green first gets darker and finally turns yellow, and the leaves begin to fall. Lastly, winter arrives, all gray and brown, the Earth strips and many trees remain bare. In the country, nobody worries about these changes. They are normal. For those who live in contact with the Earth, this becomes a lesson that is taught and learned naturally. It is the rhythm of life. It is considered normal that every season gives its fruit. Should we then be surprised that, in so-called primitive cultures, where there is strong contact with Earth, topics like aging or death are experienced with much less anxiety and worry compared to us Westerners? For them, the changes are normal. They are part of life.

On the other hand, for civilizations where contact with nature is less dramatic, it is more difficult to accept the passage of the seasons; the physical and emotional changes of aging become difficult. Often, everything possible is done to desperately color everything the green of spring—but it is not possible.

Nature has always been witness to the meeting of man and spirit in every tradition, from Indian yogi to Christian mystics like Saint Francis, to Buddhist monks, to Native Americans. This connection is so strong that it is perceived, to some degree, by all human beings, even by those less prone to spiritual issues. Otherwise, why would we escape to the outdoors as soon as possible, often confronting hours of traffic to do so? Why would we seek a spot, even if small, of green around us? Why would we fill our patios with plants?

Even unaware of these deep motivations, evidently we perceive them at the unconscious level. As soon as we can, we escape from the stress and from the concrete of the city, to seek refuge at the beach, the mountain or the lake returning, like our ancestors, to the healing power of Mother Earth. It is in nature that we find quiet and serenity.

GOING BACK HOME

"It's scary to think that, in the course of our daily lives, we have forgotten that a relationship with nature is crucial." Sally is shocked.

In effect, it is difficult to not notice the tragic parallel between the uneducated and violent way that we often treat nature and everything that is happening in the world.

In ancient India, writings suggested five precepts or acts to complete daily for spiritual evolution. The fifth (Bhuta yana) regards serving all forms of life, including animals and plants, as the incarnation of the divine essence. In those days, families would never eat before feeding the birds and domestic animals, watering the plants and even the trees around the house. To adore nature was an integral part of human life.

Often it's just before a sunset, a starry sky, a snowy mountain, the smell of the ocean or the woods that even the most skeptical human is touched by the beauty and is able to deeply feel it in his skin and let his heart fill with peace.

"Yes, in those moments, it's like we were in contact with God. I like to think of nature as the earthly manifestation of the divine." Lenny had a very serene expression. And to think that only a couple of month ago, he defined himself as an atheist.

He is right. In nature we can see ourselves more clearly, and if we want to transform something within ourselves, the best way is to start is to spend the most time possible alone in the middle of nature. The day we stop considering nature merely as a resource to exploit and we start paying more attention to its wisdom, then we will be able to use its great healing power.

In some aboriginal tribes, when the rice does not grow well, the women crouch in the field and tell the legend of the origin of rice. Then the rice remembers its purpose and starts to grow again.

We are like the rice; nature helps us remember the significance of our existence, and, if we know how to listen, a sense of unity and expansion will be evoked.

A beautiful practice that a woman of the Tigua tribe taught me is to talk to Mother Nature. It is a very easy exercise and very powerful at the same time. Many tribes consider nature as a mother. So nature becomes a safe place that holds and sustains us. It is where we can free ourselves of pain. All you need to do is go into the woods alone and start to tell Mother Nature what is bothering you or what hurts you, like I did the day my father died. The benefits are immediate; you'll feel empty, lighter and more peaceful.

"It's true," confirmed Lenny. "At the beginning, I was embarrassed. I was worried that someone would see me. I thought that, for a man my age, these things were not appropriate. Then one day, I decided to stop worrying about it and did it. I found it to be spontaneous, as if Earth had always been there waiting for me. In the end, there was only peace. I felt at home."

In fact, wasn't our first home nature? When we consciously accept this, we feel comfortable wherever destiny takes us. When this sensation of belonging to Earth is well-rooted in us, we can allow ourselves to face the storms because our roots are strong and deep.

LET'S CLEAN UP NATURE

I particularly like this practice. For me, it's like a little gift for Mother Earth to thank her for her presence. In addition, it greatly helps me to regenerate when I feel that my obligations risk devouring my energy.

Take at least a half hour (better a whole day) and go into nature with plastic bags and gloves. While you're walking in silence, pick up all the trash that you find from cigarette butts to plastic. Think of it as symbolically cleaning up all the trash in your life and as energetic cleansing. You will feel a deep contact with Mother Earth, and you will see the benefits in your daily life.

It's very nice to do this in a group—especially if you all remain silent.

ANIMALS: A SOURCE OF LOVE

It's more important to prevent an animal from suffering than to sit contemplating the evils of the universe while praying with priests.

—Buddha

"I realize that, during these years, I have toughened. My main thoughts are worries about work, money and health. It's difficult for me to feel love. Maybe I don't even know what I want to say. I feel so alone now that the children are off on their own…" Before Sally goes even deeper into what a victim she is, I interrupt her.

I heard a beautiful story about the animal world told by Native American Indians. The myth tells that in ancient times, when the world was created, a deal was made between people and animals. In the deal, the animals took the job of serving humans every way possible, even if it cost them their life. Humans, on their side, solemnly promised to protect and nourish their brothers of the animal world. Shortly after, however, the humans forgot their promise. The animals did not. They are still honoring their commitment to us.

In his book *Healing*, Professor Servan-Schreiber, affirmed neuro-psychiatrist and author of successful books, says that the medicine he most voluntarily prescribes to those who live alone is to adopt an animal.

Researchers have discovered that whoever lives with an animal is more protected against depression and shows more psychological resistance when confronted with difficulty.

Some years back, at the University of Buffalo, he conducted a study that makes one think: a large group of stock brokers suffered from hypertension and extreme stress. Half of them were given traditional medicine and half were encouraged to get a dog or a cat, depending on their preference. It only took six months to see the results: the medicine temporarily lowered the blood pressure but did not stop the spiking of it during stress, while the owners of animals demonstrated more capacity to manage the stress and interpersonal relationships, had more mental clarity and more calculating speed. Above all of this, their blood pressure remained stable even in moments of overwork.

Another research study published in the *American Journal of Cardiology* demonstrated that among people who had had heart attacks, the owners of a domestic animal had six times less probability to die during the year following the attack as those who did not have one. "For a long time, I thought that I did not need anyone or anything. Now I understand that maybe closing my heart to the world was a strategy to feel less embarrassed about having been abandoned." Sally began to understand.

When I asked if her strategy had been useful, she answered, "Well, I isolated myself. I saw people, but I never let anyone get close to the real me; I only showed a part of myself, one side, dressed and made-up. I thought I could live well even without love…"

It is not true. We cannot live without love. We can live without a sentimental relationship, but love is a biological need for us humans, as has been confirmed by many leading figures in modern science.

In this regard, Professor Servan-Schreiber explains that one of the substantial differences between reptiles and mammals is that mammals' offspring are very vulnerable and are unable to live without constant care. The most extreme case is human beings, the offspring that need the most care for the longest time. For this reason, evolution created a brain structure in us that makes us very sensitive to the needs of our children. Through this instinct, we are driven to feed them, caress them and protect them.

This mental programming is particularly strong and powerful since it was conceived to assure a relationship of love—indispensable for the survival of the species. It is exactly this need-capacity inherent in human beings that is at the base of our existence and our relationships, not only with our children but even with others. The need to give and receive love is, in fact, one of the fundamental needs in Maslow's pyramid. If, like Sally, we negate this need for long, we end up drying up our energy.

A relationship with animals allows us to train daily for love and compassion; an animal does not judge.

Its love for us does not depend on our social position, on our physical appearance or on the intelligence of what we say. An animal loves us and accepts us just as we are and teaches us to be ourselves and to open our heart. Obviously, the same can be done by directing your love toward other human beings doing volunteer work or helping the elderly or children. One does not exclude the other. Indeed, as we have seen, the more we use our capacity to love, the more we fill our life with passion (love in action).

It's not true that an animal can't live in an apartment. Certainly, if it had a garden, it would be better. But a cat or dog is definitely better in 500 square feet that in a cage at the shelter. We are not being selfish by bringing them into our home; we are selfish if we abandon them to their destiny.

In Theravada Buddhism, the kind practiced in Thailand and a good part of Southeast Asia, it is said that every good deed gives us what we deserve. So, in Thailand, even the poorest share their food with monks or with whomever has less than they do. They call it *merit-making*, doing good deeds.

To take care of a wounded or homeless animal, besides bringing love and positive emotions into our own life, produces merits. If you really can't take an animal into your home, you certainly can regularly visit a shelter. You, who live with an animal, know what I'm talking about. Animals are a wealth of pure unconditional love. Having one is like having an everlasting battery of warmth and affection.

I think that this is the commitment they made and are continuing to honor. Are we ready to honor and accept their love?

PHYSICAL EXERCISE

> *Keeping your body in good health is a must...*
> *Otherwise you are not able to keep a clear and*
> *incisive mind.*
>
> —*Buddha*

Professor Servan-Schreiber, who for years directed the neurocognitive science laboratory of Pittsburgh, told of many occasions in which his team resolved cases of anxiety and chronic depression simply with physical exercise. The cure is simple: no medicines but jogging, or simple fast walking, practice regularly from twenty to thirty minutes a day three times a week. The results were certain, so much so that the chapter in which the experiences were described was entitled "Prozac or Adidas?"

In the avant-garde of the scientific world, dozens of research programs have come to the same conclusion. It appears that whoever does physical exercise is more protected against crises of anxiety and fear—and even their immune system works better.

The first defense that the organism uses against any kind of attack is the NK (*natural killer*) cells, whose job is to neutralize external invasions like the AIDS virus and internal ones like the spread of cancer. The cells, explains Servan-Schreiber himself, appear very sensitive to the emotions: the happier we are and the better we feel, the more we work with energy. On the contrary, in periods of stress and depression, the cells tend to deactivate and to rest, stopping their protection of the organism. Physical exercise stimulates the production of endorphin, or endogen morphine, the so-called molecule of well being. It is produced by the brain and has effects similar to that of opiates producing and improving the biochemical equilibrium. This helps us escape the constant flow of thoughts and interrupts the negative spirals of the mind in a natural manner.

As Tony Buzan sustains in his book *The Thought of the Body*, "Exercising the brain positively influences the body and exercising the body positively influences the brain."

It appears that physical exercise not only cures anxiety and depression but also helps prevent them. The studies by Servan-Shreiber show that, in a population of normal subjects, those who practiced sports early in life had much less probability of suffering from anxiety or depression. This protective effect lasted for at least the next twenty-five years.

"I signed up at a gym but I quit right away, partly because it was way too much work and partly for lack of time. I did not even finish my whole membership," protested Sally.

These studies agree that it is not necessary to overdo physical exercise. The important thing is that it is done regularly. Apparently, it seems that the efficiency is due to continuity and, not, for example, by the distance run or the intensity of the work. According to more than one source, the minimum necessary is twenty minutes three times a week. It can be jogging or aerobics but even a brisk walk, swimming, biking, Yoga, Qi gong or Pilates will do.

It's true that five times a week would be better, but it is just as true that, if you are out of shape, it will do no good to throw yourself into an hour of intense exercise to end up exhausted and, more than likely, with a sense of failure and inadequacy. We would risk giving up, like Sally. The idea, instead, is to start gradually, with gentleness letting the body guide us.

FOOD FOR THE MIND

Our diet has a great effect on our character.

—*Mata Amritanandamayi*

"It's really hard for me to concentrate and often I have no energy. I have mood swings as well," tells Sally as she nervously chews her pen.

Sometimes distraction, stress, mental exhaustion or the tendency to constantly have negative thoughts, comes from the way in which we nourish our brain.

If we had to build a boat, would we not choose the best materials for navigation? When we get gas, don't we make sure that it's the best grade for our car? And for our vehicle on earth, our body, what fuel do we give? Which substances do we choose to nourish our cells and our mind?

People who claim that it's enough to have a balanced diet to get all the nutrients we need obviously have a garden and an orchard in an uncontaminated place and eat only that which they have just picked.

Even if your diet is balanced, most land nowadays has been so overplanted and overworked that produce no longer has the quantity of minerals and vitamins that we need. To eat them is important, but it's not enough for the optimal functioning of the mind-body system.

In the same way, it's good to pay lots of attention to everything that we eat. Most of the food that is found at the market contains many preservatives, artificial colorants and chemical additives. Imagine that at least ten per cent of those alimentary additives are really for conservation of the food and ninety per cent are known as "cosmetic" additives: colors, emulsions, thickeners and sweeteners. In industrialized countries, people eat between fifteen and twenty pounds of additives every year.

A simple ham sandwich contains no less than thirteen additives including emulsifiers, treating agents, stabilizers and regulators of acidity.

"And if we choose orange juice?" dared Sally.

Well, on the average, that drink contains 8 percent of orange juice and the rest is glucose-fructose syrup, sugar, aspartame and saccharine, preservatives, aromas and coloring.

You can imagine the effect that all these substances have on our body over the long term, not to mention the energy aspect. In the end, we are what we eat—even at the psychological level.

Servan-Schreiber explains that sixty per cent of the brain is made of acidic fats that are the principal components of the cerebral membrane, where most of the communication between the brain and the rest of the body happens. Since even brain cells are regenerating their components constantly, it is absolutely necessary to furnish them with fatty acids in the form of Omega 3, which is not produced by the human body but can be found in fish oil and oil of the linen seed.

In the last ten years, much research has been done on polyunsaturated fats. Apparently, in addition to being able to normalize emotional brain functioning and therefore a potent antidepressant and stabilizer of mood, they can also have multiple benefits on the heart, the skin and joints.

FOOD AND MOOD

Dan Baker, who for years has studied the relationship between food and mood, suggests daily doses of lecithin (5000-10,000 mg), vitamin C (1000-2000 mg) and B5 (100 mg). This would help to produce acetylcholine which activates communication between the neurons.

It appears that vitamins C and E are among the most important nutrients for mood; magnesium and calcium are for remaining calm; chromium is to stabilize sugar in the blood; and the complex vitamin B, especially B12 for energy, niacin against anxiety and B6 and folic acid for preventing depression. This last element also explains why, when we are down in the dumps, we crave chocolate; it is rich in folic acid.

In addition, if you haven't already done it, consult a good homeopath, naturopath or trusted doctor to discover whether you have allergies or intolerances to any food. They can strongly influence your mood and your ability to completely utilize your capacities.

"What do you think about eating meat?" Sally wants to know. "I really like it."

Recently I found a cartoon on the internet: "Vegetarians are strange people—Hippocrates, Gandhi, Darwin, Einstein, Freud, Galileo, Kafka, Leonardo da Vinci, Martin Luther King, Newton, Pythagoras, Seneca, Plato, Wagner, Tolstoy, Voltaire…" I think the fact that so many people who have so strongly contributed so much to the progress of humanity and have made this choice makes you think. Personally, I've been a vegetarian since I was ten years old and vegan for the last nine years. If I think of the fear that the animals have at the moment they are killed and to the continued suffering that we cause them today making them live in horrible conditions, without even space enough to move, I am ashamed to be a "human being." In the United States alone, 660,000 animals are killed every hour for human consumption, and, in Europe, it's not much better.[17]

The fear and suffering of the killed animal, in the form of adrenaline, in addition to the hormones and various toxic substances, is emitted into your body when you eat meat.

In his book *Eco-cide,* Professor Jeremy Rifkin states that the phenomenon of "mad cow" is a clear symptom that something is not working as it should be in the food chain.

---

[17] If you would like more information on this fact, you can visit various sites on veganism from which much of this information was sourced.

And this is probably also true for the most recent outbreak of avian flu.

Moreover, researchers at the University of Oxford found that cutting animal products from your diet could reduce an individual's carbon footprint from food by up to 73 percent. In fact, livestock and their byproducts are responsible for 51 percent of all worldwide greenhouse emissions, more than the combined exhaust from all transportation.[18]

So eating a vegan diet could be the "single biggest way" to reduce your environmental impact on earth.

On top of that, several scientific studies have amply demonstrated the influence of diet on character. It was discovered that those who regularly consume red meat tend to have more aggressive reactions and that refined sugars deplete the body of precious vitamins and minerals, producing a condition of hyperacidity. This, in time, induces sleepiness, difficulty concentrating, irritability and loss of mnemonic ability. In other words, it makes the mind still more unstable and diminishes its potential. To regularly eat food rich in these substances is like giving your computer a virus.

Despite all this, I am not inviting you to become a vegan or even a vegetarian. I believe in it and it is definitely what I follow, but I am also convinced that everyone must choose for themselves.

It is, however, decidedly a call to be more aware of the material with which you build your boat because it will definitely make a difference during your journey. I strongly invite you to document all the possibilities that the marketplace offers. Experiment for yourself or, better yet, with the help of a professional. You can get real help.

---

[18] *Livestock's Long Shadow: environmental issues and options.* Food and Agriculture Organization of the United Nations, Rome, 2006.

To change your diet means to leave your comfort zone, to modify a very deep and consolidated habit. To do this also makes it necessary to makes changes in other areas of your life as well.

Working Teams: Blue or Red Pill

> *It seems that everybody has the exact idea of how we should live our life. But they never know how to live their own.*
>
> —*Paulo Coelho*

"I am a bit embarrassed about it, but when Lenny began this journey, I really opposed it," confessed Sally. "I saw him change and it scared me. Now I realize that I was afraid for myself, not for him. His change made me have to face all my issues. One day, he came to visit and when, as usual, I complained about my situation, he told me to stop playing the victim and to take responsibility for my life. I could choose! I just could not accept this concept. I got very angry. This was not the Lenny I knew. I tried to discourage him from attending the courses and, since he did not listen to me, I stopped talking to him." Sally now laughs at herself. This was an excellent sign.

Lenny smiles too when he remembers. "It was not an easy time. After Laura died, Sally was always my rock and not having her support was difficult. As if that was not enough, I was not comfortable with my old friends any more. Often, I felt like someone who gets on the wrong escalator at the mall at the busiest hour of the day at Christmas time. I tried to go up, but everyone was coming down and telling me that I was making a mistake. And at some moments, I thought that they were right, that I should have left my path and followed the crowd."

As soon as we enter the road toward change, we are in a very particular and delicate phase. We are leaving an old state and haven't yet reached a new one. We are letting go of dysfunctional habits and consolidated behaviors, and we are giving life to a new identity. Just like a pregnant woman is always careful of her condition, aware of where she goes and with whom, and careful to keep her unborn child out of danger, we, too, must be aware of the change that is happening in us and protect it, at least, until it is born. A seed can easily be stepped on by anyone in the area and our dreams can be suffocated by people around us. But when the seed grows and becomes a tree with deep roots and strong branches, it can't be knocked down even by punching it or by cutting it with a pair of scissors. In other words, once the transformation has happened and the new identity, beliefs and behaviors are well-established, we are able to face any situation much more easily.

Roberto Assagioli, father of psycho-synthesis, in his book *The Phases of the Process of Transmutation: Spiritual Development and Neuro-psychic Disturbances,* published in 1933, wrote, "Spiritual growth is a condition similar to that of caterpillars that are going through the process of transforming into butterflies. They must pass through the phase of chrysalis, which is a condition of disintegration and impotence.

But man, in general, does not have the privilege of the caterpillar, which makes the change while protected by and surrounded by its cocoon.

Man must, especially today, continue to conduct his daily life and do his best to carry out his family, professional and social obligations as if nothing were happening to him. The hard problem that he must resolve is similar to what English engineers would have to do if they were to transform and enlarge a grand railroad station in London without interrupting traffic for even one hour."

Do you feel like those engineers?

Often, we have the sensation that it's our family, our friends and colleagues that are afraid of our transformation. It is known that change is scary, and, as we have seen, risks destabilizing the current order, the equilibrium that, whether false or dangerous, has worked up to now and that often involves them.

When I left my job as a model, and, as a result, also abandoned the companies that I had created in the world of fashion, the modeling agency and the fashion show organizing company, for a while, I was told by my friends and colleagues that I was crazy. And they said it with the best of intentions. They loved me and were afraid for me. Probably they were afraid that I would end up living under a bridge or lost on some Indian beach. They were animated by good intention, but I needed to take that step for my own evolution and to activate my true mission in life. Most of them could not understand. My husband, Nicola, before getting involved in training, was a lawyer. Born into a family of lawyers, he had a great position in one of the best law firms in Milan. When he chose to change jobs and dedicate his life to the development of human potential, we did not know each other yet, but he told me of the difficulties that he had to overcome.

Most of the people close to him tried to discourage him. They tried to protect him from possible mistakes. In their matrix of the world, to leave a job, a solid and fruitful profession, was very risky and should not be done. "Sometimes I felt like I was the star in the movie *matrix* when he had to choose between the red pill and the blue one. On one hand, there was the imaginary world and, on the other, the search for his own truth…"

Lenny joked about the difficulty he had to face.

If you have begun the journey toward personal growth, probably you have stopped being bound by the dictates of society and of advertisements; you have stopped feeling guilty if your body is not that of a model, if you have wrinkles or if your family is not that of *Leave it to Beaver* or *The Brady Bunch*.

Maybe you're trying to escape the circle of fear that we feel when we read the newspaper or listen to the TV, or maybe you have decided to stop believing that the world is made only of soccer players, movie stars, terrorism, floods, disease, accidents, violence and murders. Just by writing this, I felt my breathing stop and probably my immune system was weakened as well as my mood changed. This is a clear example of the type of conditionings to get away from. That is not all the world is made of.

Probably, over time, you have ended up feeling different. Certainly you have had to deal with people who have tried to bring you into the conditionings of the matrix, to induce you to follow the laws of consumerism, to hide your own uniqueness. And maybe, to not feel left out or to not lose your friends, you are ready to betray yourself. Don't do it. As Marianne Williamson writes, there is nothing enlightening about shrinking yourself to the point where you make those around you uncomfortable. Playing small does not help the world.

CREATE COMMUNITY

All you have to do is strengthen your new identity. "That's all, but how?" asks Sally. "How can we find people who support us in the change, that speak our language?"

"Like here in the course," echoes Lisa.

It will help you a great deal to have a group of people with whom you can share the path of change. It will also help to continually use the tools of change.

Obviously, you must form a group of individuals that have a vision and a clear and, better yet, a shared goal. To be clear, it won't work if the goal of half of the group is to grow, meditate or practice the exercises in this book and the other half comes to the meetings to play cards or to just hang out. And it won't work either if you think that the group is there just to satisfy your needs or to give you help but you're not willing to listen and to give your support to others. If this is the case, you probably will never find the right group.

It's been years now that, all over the world in various contexts, from corporations to hospitals to organizations, this type of support group has been working well. And the reason is obvious. Think about it: one of the basic principles of a meeting of emotions is that if we share joy, it increases; yet if we share pain, it decreases!

During the tsunami, I was in Phuket and I quickly went to the hospital to help. We, volunteers, were divided into groups and sent wherever help was needed. For a few days, I worked together with Al, a distinguished American man who had no experience helping people. At the beginning, I was doubtful; the situation was difficult. We had to deal with wounds, often very serious, and with people who had lost everything, their job, their house and their family. What would Al do?

Within the first ten minutes, I was shocked and ashamed of my stupid assumptions. Al was wonderful. His great talent was being able to listen, with his heart, to dozens of people, adults and children, all in a state of shock. His love for people, his generosity and his incredible humanity deeply moved me, and, upon going home, every night, when I thought of him, I imagined an angel. There is no need to be particularly prepared, to have degrees or specific classes before you are able to help others. It certainly was not in such an extreme case as that, so imagine how easy it would be in daily life. All you need to do is find others like yourself who honestly want to improve and make evolutionary changes. The important thing is that, within the group, you are a willing to share dreams and emotions, to overcome fear and conditionings and to support and listen to one another without judging.

One of the goals of this book is to create a long-lasting community of people who can meet autonomously, create groups, and support each other in reaching their goals and in their personal improvement.

For this I created a community on Facebook called "A Whole New Life, Lucia Giovannini" where you will see various sections dedicated to this long-term mission, and you will find information about how to get in contact with other people in your area. As you desire, you can complete the exercises in this book and the others suggested on the site together; you can discuss your experiences and help each other—perhaps even go to the movies or grab a meal together. The journey to change, connect, and grow within your new community will allow you all to create A Whole New Life together. It is my wish, that your Whole New Life community meets in your city or in your neighborhood and creates a profound ripple effect in your communities that inspires everyone to gather with love, light and abundance. Remember that we support you, too!

We, as Bless You International, will try to continue to provide you with new ideas for reflection, new exercises, and new information about various ideas to help you bring constant improvements to your life. You will find everything you need on my website: www.luciagiovannini.com.

And, if you want, we can furnish you with a coach or a Bless You International trainer who will follow the group that you have created. You can also attend the courses that we regularly organize all around the world uniting you with many friends of Bless You International

In other words, there are infinite possibilities to create together a great community of new men and women.

The concept of community throughout the centuries has always had a fundamental role. Community is not a place in which we exchange only hospitality and help; it is also a group that recognizes our talents and pushes us to discover the purpose in our lives. By way of this type of group, we can recognize our gifts and offer them to the world.

"Speaking of world," interjected Sally, "how would things change in all the relationships, in both family and in work, if we lived according to these principles? How would it be if the world were a lot of groups connected to one another all sharing this philosophy? Would it not be marvelous?"

"It is my dream! It's because of this that I brought you here!" responded Lenny.

It is my dream, too. And I am very happy to share it with you.

IN THE END

*This is not the end, but it is not the beginning
either. It is only the end of the beginning.*

—*Sally and Lisa, at the end of the course*

THE LAST DAN

*To improve is to change. To be
perfect is to change often.*

—*Winston Churchill*

If I understand correctly, there are four basic steps for evolutionary change: the first is to listen to the calling for change, understand where we are and what contents of the matrix block us. The second is to clarify where we want to go. It means establishing clear and highly motivating goals that are part of our purpose for living and that express our values and for which we are passionate. The third is to prepare ourselves using the tools of transformation and the seven steps of the vision. The fourth is to take action, remembering the various phases that we must cross in the process of change." Sally tried to summarize what she had learned in her pragmatic style.

"Is that right?" she added while I was still thinking of how to respond.

Yes, it is like that, even though it is not such a straight line as it seems. We are used to thinking that after point one, there is point two and then point three. But human beings are much more complex. Within us, there are many processes all happening at the same time, so it is necessary to think in a systemic manner.

In Theravala Buddhism, the road to interior evolution is called the triple path. It is about three practices: *panna* or awareness or comprehension, *sila* which means purification and, finally, *samadhi* which is intense concentration.

Panna, sila and *samadhi* work in a systemic way, in a kind of spiral.

"I don't understand. What does that have to do with us?" asks Sally curiously.

If you had not developed clear awareness of the need for change, you would not be here. Maybe, thanks to this new information, you will want to modify your behaviors, do the suggested exercises and attend the courses. Through these practices, you will begin to experience more concentration. Your mind, usually very agitated, will begin to quiet. In this way you can develop more awareness. This better understanding will help you to better see the impurities in your mind-body system in terms of limiting beliefs, behaviors, emotions, dysfunctional habits and old not-yet-forgiven grudges. This will push you to purify yourself and to let go. When the purification has happened, you will have more space, time and energy to use the tools for change. All this will only increase your awareness. And so on.

The steps toward evolutionary change function in the same way, always systematically.

Portia Nelson, an American singer and actress of the last century, left us a beautiful brief autobiography in five chapters. I don't think there's anything that better illustrates the path of evolutionary change:

> *"Chapter one; I walk along a street. There's a deep hole in the sidewalk. I fall in. I am lost. I can't do anything. It's not my fault. It takes me a lifetime to get out.*
>
> *Chapter two; I walk along a street. There's a deep hole in the sidewalk. I pretend that it's not there. I fall in. I can't believe that I'm back in the same spot. It's not my fault. But it's takes a long time to get out.*
>
> *Chapter three; I walk along a street. There's a deep hole in the sidewalk. I see it clearly. I fall in it again. It's a habit, but my eyes are open; I know where I am. It's my fault. I get right out.*
>
> *Chapter four; I walk along a street. There's a deep hole in the sidewalk. I walk around it.*
>
> *Chapter five; I take a different street."*

The phase of solidification can last for years. Often we find ourselves faced with old problems (the usual holes) when we think we've already eliminated them. Evolutionary change is not a straight line, but proceeds according to a spiral that grows toward the top. If we think in a straight line, when the old problem shows up, we mistakenly think that we have failed and we haven't evolved. In reality, every time we meet the old pattern we face it at a superior level. It will keep showing up until we have passed it and resolved all of the facets of the situation. If you don't understand this dynamic and you think in a straight line instead of in a spiral, the risk is to believe that we are happy only once we arrive at our goal.

It isn't like that. Like in the martial arts, there is no final Dan. It's the same in life; we will never finish learning, growing, improving. This is the goal. And it is during this journey that we meet happiness as well.

CHANGING YOURSELF

> *An artist has to be careful to not get to a point that makes him believe that he has reached his destination. He must realize that there is always more to come. As long as he stays in that spot, everything is will be fine.*
>
> —*Bob Dylan,* No Direction Home

Carol Dweck, professor of psychology at Stanford, has conducted a study for over thirty years on why some people excel and some do not. The research demonstrates that the motive for success is not innate talent but the capacity to confront failure.

Dweck discovered that at the base of it all, there is an element that she called mental structure. There are two kinds: fixed or open, also known as growth. We all possess very distinctly, one or the other. It is easy to imagine which of the two leads to success.

In the matrix of self and personal power of the person who has a fixed mental structure, we find fixed characteristics and beliefs carved in stone, like "I am good," or "I am bad," ; "I am intelligent," or "I am stupid." The problem with this kind of thinking is that those who believe they are capable also believe that they don't need to improve, while those who think they are not capable think that, however hard they try, it will be useless.

"Imagine that I have a fixed mental structure, that I have always been told that I am intelligent and that I am convinced that I am capable. Isn't that a desirable situation? Is not it what we are all aiming for?" Sally has a concentrated expression on her face. Probably the concept is not clear to her.

It's a desirable situation until you find the first hole. What will happen then? Where will intelligence and capacity end up? Don't misunderstand. I'm not saying that all this is not fine on its own. But if we have a fixed mental structure and we believe ourselves to be intelligent and capable, we end up feeling obliged to never make a mistake. To defend our role, we feel obligated to demonstrate our capabilities in every occasion, and we must always be ready to achieve what is expected of us. We are not capable of confronting the holes because we see them as failures. To fall in would be proof that we are not capable, after all, and this would put our identity in crisis. It would be a huge disappointment. Not being capable would mean that we are a failure. Therefore, to avoid the risk of failure, we avoid setting ourselves up for failure, we tend to choose objectives and challenges that are easy. We try to hide our failures because it would undermine our image. And when, inevitably, we fall in the old holes, we risk abandoning our vision, or, to defend ourselves, we start to blame others.

Those who have an open mental structure, on the other hand, avoid labels and instead think of life as a series of works in progress. They don't go to the 3Ps every time they find a hole because they know that falling in a hole is an opportunity to grow.

Every hole, in fact, is a challenge to find new solutions and to push ourselves to improve. For this reason, it is important to appreciate all the effort that we exert, each new thing that we learn, even if we haven't arrived yet where we want to be—and it seems like the journey is taking forever.

To fall in the old holes is nothing more than a learning curve. This is the only way that we can slowly change ourselves.

CHANGE THE WORLD

Be the change that you want to see in the world.

—*M. K. Gandhi*

A girl complained to her father about her life and how things were so difficult. Every time a problem was solved, another came along. She did not know how to go on and was ready to give up. She was tired of fighting. Her father, a chef, took her to where he worked.

There he filled three pans with water and put them on the stove. When the water started to boil, he put some carrots in one, eggs in a second and coffee beans in the third. He let the water boil without saying a word while his daughter watched impatiently. After twenty minutes, he turned off the stove, took out the carrots and put them on a plate. He took out the eggs and put them on another plate. Finally, he took the coffee and put it in a cup.

Looking at his daughter, he said, "Dear Daughter, carrots, eggs or coffee?" The girl did not understand. He asked her to come closer and touch the carrots. She did it and noticed that they were soft. Then he asked her to take an egg and break it. While she took off the shell, she noticed that the egg was hard. Then he asked her to taste the coffee. She smiled as she enjoyed the rich aroma.

The girl still did not understand and asked, "What does all this mean?"

Here is what the man answered: "All three of these things faced the same adversity, boiling water, but each reacted differently. The carrot was strong, tough and proud and was difficult to break, but, after being put in boiling water, it became weak, soft and easy to take apart. The egg arrived at the water fragile, with a thin skin to protect its delicate insides, but, after being in the boiling water, got hard inside. The coffee beans were unique. After being put in the boiling water, they changed the water. Which one do you want to be, dear Daughter?" he asked. "When adversity knocks on your door, how will you respond?"

How do we choose to react when faced with the boiling water of life? Will we choose, as Sarah did, to be a carrot and always seem to be tough, but, when problems and pain touch us, become weak and lose all our energy?

Or will we be like Lenny and Sally, choosing to be an egg that starts out with a malleable heart and good spirit, but who, after a death, a separation, a job loss or an obstacle, becomes hard and rigid? Maybe externally they are the same, but inside they are bitter and cynical with a hardened spirit and heart.

Or do we want to be like a coffee bean? The coffee changes the water—the same thing that caused the pain—and makes it better.

* * *

Often I hear people say "I want to change the world." I, myself, often have this impulse, and I have had it forever, since I was a child. It's a noble proposition that can, however, lead to frustration at times. The world is so big; I am but a grain of sand in the desert; that which I do, say or think does not count.

This is not true. By whom is the world composed? Is it not made of nations, cities, blocks, families, offices and groups of people who have relationships with one another?

Every one of us has an impact on the world, whether we are aware or not. And when we decide to follow our dreams and to improve ourselves, we become an example for others. When we choose to be like the coffee, we spread an unmistakable aroma around us. When we carry light within us and let it shine, even when faced with difficulty, we automatically illuminate the street of those who surround us.

It is here that we stop asking ourselves what life is giving us and begin to ask what we are giving to the world. It is then that our push to contribute to the world becomes powerful. It is the hero (or heroine) who takes his lonely voyage where he beats his demons—his true conditionings and limitations—and takes the gifts he reaped out to the community. Our transformation opens new possibilities for change—even for others.

It is by changing ourselves that we can change the world around us.

"Do you have a final suggestion?" Sally wants to know after listening to everything carefully.

Continue to study, to read and to nourish yourself with inspirational texts. Look for books that can give you new points of view and stimulations, biographies of people that you admire and that you want to imitate, stories that entice you and vibrate the chords of your very being the very highest possible.

The more you immerse yourself into these texts, the more chances you will have to travel new highways and to automatically choose which street is the most adapt for you. I find it hard to believe that there is only one right way. But don't trust fake gurus who pretend to be authorized by some divinity when they tell you that theirs is the only way. Don't trust those who promise illumination in a day or without hard work or those who tell you that it will be them who heal you.

If you really want to change, the results will come. But it will take time, and it is you who has to do the necessary work. Nobody can do it for you. There are no shortcuts.

When you start to get the first results, you will be tempted to attribute them to whomever guided you in the process: your therapist, your coach, your teacher. Don't do it. Certainly their support is important and it's right to acknowledge them, but it is you who walked the walk. Learn to honor yourself.

If you are therapists, coaches, trainers or spiritual teachers and the participants in your courses put you on a pedestal offering crowns of laurel, resist the temptation to believe that the crown belongs to you. That crown belongs firstly to the person who is offering it to you. That person has reopened himself to life and has learned to amplify their own resources, has reawakened love, has begun to see the beauty and the divine in the folds of existence. If you allow all of this to reflect on yourself, you are stealing the possibility for them to consolidate this transformation into their life. You won't be able to acknowledge all the qualities that they give you. Don't be greedy; don't keep the recognition for yourself; give it back to them.

Realize, experiment and discover for yourself what is true for you. Choose your path freely. And once you choose it, don't fall into the easy traps of fundamentalism. Always leave the door open so the new and different can find you and reach you.

"Do you have books to recommend? What can we read? Haven't you written anything?" asked Sally.

"There are thousands of books for sale, but, at my site, you can request a list of interesting reading...I wrote one. It's called *A Whole New Life.*"

Thank you for sharing with me, with Mark, Rosanne, Andrew and Lisa, Sarah, Lenny and Sally. And thank you for having read our stories of change.

I hope to hear yours one day.

* * *

One of the nicest sensations is the conviction to have lived life the way you wanted, with moments that were easy and those that were difficult, with the good and the bad, a life completely yours, formed by your choices and not those of others.

—*Michel Ignatieff*

Enjoy!
Lucia

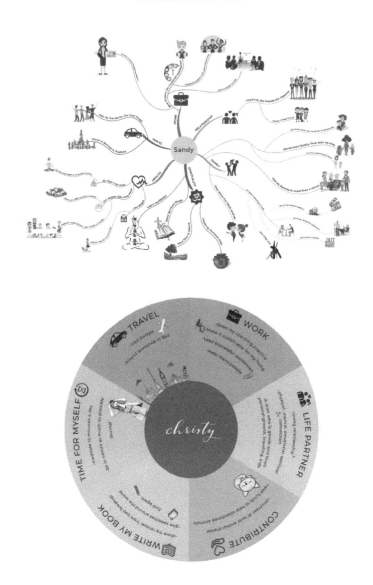

To explore your whole new life, be sure to visit luciagiovannini.com with an abundance of resources, tools, and an online experience to help guide you on your way.

ACKNOWLEDGMENTS

If we don't change, we don't grow. If we don't grow, we aren't really living.

—Gail Sheehy

To whomever asks me how long it took me to write this book, I tell the truth—my whole life. To mention all those who supported me along my journey, I would have to write a whole chapter. I apologize if I don't name you one by one. To all of you go my deepest thanks. I cannot, however, neglect to thank the people who have contributed in a more active way, and I want to do it in chronological order, according to the events that caused the birth of *A Whole New Life*.

First of all, I thank my husband, Nicola Riva, who took over most of my work with Bless You International while I was busy with the draft. I also owe him a lot for many of the ideas that made the book more complete. If in Bless You International we had a research and development area,

Nicola would definitely be the director. Thank you, Nicola, for always being a continuous stimulus for improvement.

And I want to thank the people who, besides encouraging me, offered their experience in the field and were true literary guardian angels:, Marco Garavaglia (my first agent in Italy) and Elisabetta Albieri of Sperling & Kupfer (my Italian publishing house).

Also, a heartfelt thank you to Madeline Sturgeon, Anthony Ziccardi and the entire team at Post Hill Press for having supported the project and for bringing this book to the US.

Finally, this book could not have arrived in your hands if it had not been for two special people: Annalisa Minutillo, an angel disguised as an Italian "A Whole New Life"-certified Coach, and my US agent, Steve Harris from CSG Literary Partners. Thanks Annalisa and Steve for believing in me and for your precious support. I couldn't have made it without you both.

I also want to thank Vincenzo Ciummo and Barbara Casó who gave me encouragement, counsel, and ideas of great value for the English version of this book. Thank you, Vincenzo and Barbara, for your precious support.

I also want to thank Sharon Ciummo, who not only took care of the translation, but actually brought every page of this book into her own life. Thank you, Sharon, for your passion and your perseverance.

Vincenzo, Barbara, Sharon, it is thanks to you that the English edition was born; I am immensely grateful for your help.

A special thanks to my fantastic international team and for the amazing work you are doing. In particular, thanks to Neeta Bushan, Lisa Zahran, Himanshu Jakhar, Garima Saxena, and to the Italian Bless You team, Giacomo Gardini,

Diletta Marabini, Federica Allegro, Gaia Monti, Ada Ammirata, Ilaria Martini, and Annachiara Magenta.

Thanks also to all the outstanding teachers I've met in many years: thanks to Patricia Crane and Rick Nichol for your support and for your invaluable friendship. Thanks also to the Heal Your Life teachers community—you are awesome! Thanks to Peggy Dylan and Maria Treviso for introducing me to the fire element and to the precious Native American culture. Thanks to Michael Hall, Michelle Duval and the whole Neuro-Semantics Community for being such an inspiration for me and to Derek Sivers, Alessandro Giuliani, Sneha Shah, Shashank Gupta for your enthusiastic feedback on the book. It meant a lot to me.

During the writing and rewriting of the various chapters, I received great and loving assistance from the participants in my courses and, in particular, from the students of the Free University of Personal Growth, who, at every meeting, asked for news about the book and my progress. Thanks to all of you for filling my life with your precious presence. I have gained so much because you have allowed me into your lives and have shared your personal journeys with me.

A very special thanks to the courageous people who have decided to follow the training to become "A Whole New Life" teachers and coaches and to bring this philosophy to other people. I am so thankful for your commitment and passion.

In addition, I want to honor the authors of the books that have inspired and stimulated me. In reality, during all these years, there are so many ideas that influenced me, so much research that enthused me and so many intuitions that I shared, that it is no longer possible to establish to whom I am in debt for which idea and in which form.

Finally, I thank you who have read the book. Thanks for bringing evolutionary change into your life and, by doing this, for helping the world be a better place.

BIBLIOGRAPHY

Alpert, Richard (Ram Dass), *Paths to God, Living the BhagavadGita*, Harmony books, New York 2004.

—, *Cambiamenti*, Corbaccio, Milano 2005.

Anolli, Luigi, Legrenzi, Paolo, *Psicologia generale*, Il Mulino, Bologna 2006.

Artress, Lauren, *Walking a Sacred Path*, Riverhead Books, 2006.

Assagioli, Roberto, *Le fasi del processo di trasmutazione*, Astrolabio, Roma 1933.

Austin, James, *Zen and the Brain*, MIT Press, Cambridge 1998.

Baker, Dan E Stauth, Cameron, *Voglio essere felice*, Piemme, Casale Monferrato 2004.

Bennett-Goleman, Tara, *Alchimia emotiva*, BUR, Milano 2002.

Buzan, Tony, *Il pensiero del corpo*, Frassinelli, Milano 1985.

—, *Usiamo la testa*, Frassinelli, Milano 1986.

—, *Embracing Change*, BBC Books, 2006.

Comaford-Lynch, Christine, *Rules for Renegades*, McGraw-Hill Companies, 2007.

Covey, Stephen R., *Le sette regole per avere successo*, Franco Angeli, Milano 2005.

Csikszentmihalyi, Mihaly, *Buon business*, Il Sole 24 Ore, Milano 2007.

Frankl, Victor, Alla ricerca di un significato della vita, Mursia, Milano 1974.

Garfinkel, Perry, *Alla ricerca del Buddha*, Sonzogno, Milano 2007.

Goleman, Daniel, *Intelligenza sociale*, Rizzoli, Milano 2006.

Hall, Michael, *Motivation, how to be a positive force in a negative world*, Good news encounters, Grand Junction 1987.

—, *Secrets of Personal Mastery*, Crown House Publishing, Carmarthen 2000.

—, *Matrix Model*, Neuro-Semantic Publications, 2002.

—, *Figuring Out People*, Crown House Publishing, 2006.

—, *Unleashed*, Neuro-Semantic Publications, 2007.

Hall, Michael, Duval, Michelle E Dilts, Robert, *Coaching Conversations 1 & 2*, Crown House Publishing, 2005.

Hamel, Gary, *Leader della Rivoluzione*, Il Sole 24 Ore, Milano 2004.

Katz, Richard, *Boiling Energy*, Harvard University Press, Cambridge 1982.

Knight, Sue, *NLP at work*, NB Editions. LAYARD, RICHARD, *Felici*tà, Rizzoli, Milano 2005.

Maslow, *Motivazione e personali*tà, Armando Editore, Roma 2006.

Muller, Wayne, *Sabbath*, Sounds True, 2007.

Ricard, Matthieu, *Il gusto di essere felici*, Sperling & Kupfer, Milano 2008.

Rifkin, James, *Ecocidio*, Mondadori, Milano 2002.

Seligman, Martin E.P., *La costruzione della felici*tà, Sperling & Kupfer, Milano 2003.

—, *Imparare l'ottimismo*, Giunti, Firenze 2005.

Servan-Schreiber, David, *Guarire*, Sperling & Kupfer, Milano 2003.

Somé, Malidoma, Patrice, *La saggezza guaritrice dell'Africa*, Il Punto d'Incontro, Vicenza 2000.

Walsh, Roger E Vaughan, Frances, *Paths Beyond Ego*, Jeremy P. Tarcher, 1993.

Wexler, Bruce E., *Brain and culture*, MIT Press, Cambridge 2006.

Wilber, Ken, *A brief history of everything*, Shambhala Publications, Boston 2007.

Wolf, Margaret, *In sweet company*, Lotus Press, 2002.

Zander, Benjamin E Zander, Rosamund, *L'arte del possibile*, Il Sole 24 Ore, Milano 2004, 318.

ABOUT THE AUTHOR

Lucia Giovannini holds a Doctorate in Psychology and Counseling and a Bachelor in Psycho-Anthropology, and is an International Affiliate of the American Psychological Association. She is also a Master Fire-walking Trainer, a Master Breathwork Trainer, an NLP and Neuro-Semantics Trainer, a certified Coach and the Western Europe Veriditas Labyrinth facilitator's coordinator. Lucia is the certified Heal Your Life® trainer for Italy and has been defined as "the Italian Louise Hay" by prestigious media like *Marie France Asia*, *The Times of India*, and *La Stampa*.

She is the founder at BlessYou International, and co-director at LUCE (Free University of Evolutionary Growth). She has been teaching courses and at conferences for about twenty-five years now to individuals and companies all over Europe and Asia.

Her work crafts a synergy between traditional psychological techniques, motivational practices, and ancient rituals that turns her seminars into something truly unique. She is often sought after by groups and companies because of her powerful seminars and she is well known for the clarity, sincerity, and inspiration of her exceptional work. For more information, visit www.luciagiovannini.com.